Patterns in pocket.

Marie Osmond's
Heartfelt Giving
sew and quilt for family and friends

Martingale®
& COMPANY

CREDITS

President & CEO: Tom Wierzbicki

Editor in Chief: Mary V. Green

Managing Editor: Tina Cook

Developmental & Technical Editor: Karen Costello Soltys

Copy Editor: Sheila Chapman Ryan

Design Director: Stan Green

Production Manager: Regina Girard

Illustrator: Laurel Strand

Cover & Text Designer: Shelly Garrison

Photographer: Douglas Carter of DC Snaps

MISSION STATEMENT

Dedicated to providing quality products and service to inspire creativity.

Marie Osmond's Heartfelt Giving: Sew and Quilt for Family and Friends
© 2010 by Marie Osmond

That Patchwork Place® is an imprint of Martingale & Company®.

Martingale & Company
19021 120th Ave. NE, Suite 102
Bothell, WA 98011 USA
www.martingale-pub.com

Printed in China
15 14 13 12 11 10   8 7 6 5 4 3 2 1

Library of Congress Cataloging-in-Publication Data is available upon request.

ISBN: 978-1-56477-947-2

Dedication

To my Grandmothers, who loved to sew,
embroider, crochet, and quilt, and who were
willing to try every other type of crafting to
bring joy and beauty into their homes and
into the homes of loved ones. I cherish the
legacy they passed down to my mother and
me. Now it's up to us to pass it on
for future generations to enjoy!

Contents

I've sometimes joked about how, when I was a 16-year-old girl on the original *Donny and Marie* show, Bob Mackie, our Emmy award–winning designer, would make my wardrobe from the yards and yards of fabric he had left over from Cher's sparely designed costumes.

Even though there isn't any truth to that wardrobe fable, my mother probably would have agreed that using leftover fabric was a very good idea. After all, my mom grew up under the "waste not, want not" philosophy of the generation that lived through the Great Depression. Throughout her entire life, my mother loved fabrics of all varieties, and treated them more like a lavish gift that she was fortunate to have than an everyday practicality.

When my brothers were young, she would go to the fabric store and pick out a bolt of fabric to make them all matching shirts. She didn't do that necessarily for the cuteness factor of seven boys dressed alike, but because buying a bolt of fabric was simply cheaper than purchasing yardage of multiple fabrics and, with a big family, frugality was a must!

Little did my brothers know that in five years they would all be wearing matching Elvis-style white rhinestone jumpsuits on stage. Ah, the '70s!

When my four oldest brothers started performing as a young barbershop quartet, it was actually the look-alike fabric that helped them stand out on the streets of Disneyland, where they were first discovered for *The Andy Williams Show*. In essence, it was my mom's love of material and her homemade matching button-down shirts that became the ticket needed to kick off the greatest ride our family could imagine (although I doubt my oldest brother, Virl, was thrilled about dressing identical to Jay, who was 11 years younger). Most likely my mother, who worked for the War Department as an efficiency expert, thought it was a perfect way to always be able to quickly locate her children at any event.

When I came along, as child number eight and her first and only girl, the sewing machine rarely cooled down. She couldn't wait for the chance to make me little dresses with added frills. To this day, I have a difficult time with anything pink! When I sculpted my first doll in the likeness of my mother, I purposely dressed her in *blue!*

Growing up in a family of singers, our home was always filled with music. However, one of the most comforting sounds that defined my childhood was the hum of the sewing machine. My mother radiated pure joy when she was busy with a new sewing project. Quilting was one of her favorite ways to spend any spare time (which she didn't have much of) and quilts were her favorite gift to give to those she loved. She had a lighthearted "bet" with her close girlfriends, who also sewed and crafted. She would claim with a wink: "Whoever dies with the most fabric wins!" After she passed away, I passed along her fabrics to other family members and friends. There was so much of it that I know she won!

I was mesmerized while going through my mom's many storage containers of fabrics and bins full of "fat quarters" that she had collected over the decades. As I sorted through her collection hour after hour, I would imagine her choosing to buy each particular print, and how she might have daydreamed about what she would make with it: an apron, a tablecloth, a tote bag, or most likely, a quilt. My daughter, who was going through my mother's storage containers with me, declared that the fabrics were "retro cool." I have to ask: Can they be called "retro" if they were the originals from the 1970s?

One of my older daughters, who loves crafting, received her grandmother's well-worn sewing machine. It was unfortunately lost in my house fire in 2005, along with some of my mother's handmade items, which had great sentimental value to me. A few of these items were saved, though, and I still have the priceless memories of the many times I was by my mother's side as she sewed and patiently taught me these skills. I tell my own children about these memories whenever we work on a sewing project together.

I first learned simple hand sewing and cross-stitching as a preschooler, while touring with my performing brothers. I could sew on a button almost before I could even button up my own coat.

My first "major" craft project with my mother was a quilt we made together for my dolls when I was just five years old. My mother let me choose the fabrics I wanted to use and helped me work with the scissors to cut out the squares. I still have this first quilt I made with her; it hangs on the wall near my Janome sewing machines. Though it's a bit faded from many washings and it's obvious that the corners are frayed, I love the memories it holds for me. As you can see from the faded photograph below, I never went anywhere without a doll or 2 or 5 (okay, 25), and my dolls never went anywhere without their personal handmade quilts.

Chillin' with my dolls . . . who never got chilly under their homemade quilt.

What a huge sense of accomplishment that little 2' x 2' quilt gave me as a small girl. My mother was very wise that way. She knew that busy hands not only kept a growing mind occupied, but also encouraged my self esteem and a sense of creativity that has been amazingly helpful in every area of my life—whether I'm helping my kids with their Halloween costumes; making them all matching pajamas for Christmas (I'm sure my 26-year-old son doesn't always appreciate matching his 7-year-old sister . . . but, hey, some traditions must be maintained!); designing an album cover, handbags, or jewelry; or creating my award-winning line of collectible dolls. What a gift of love she gave to me.

As I mentioned, as a young teenager I had the unique opportunity to learn about fabrics and design from some of the best clothing designers in the world. Whenever I could slip away from the set of *Donny and Marie* or whatever show or TV special I was doing at the time, I would make my way to the studio's wardrobe department. It was intriguing to see what one-of-a-kind dresses and outfits were being created for other performers—or for me—on their very active sewing machines. I would never get tired of talking about color and design with these amazing designers and their seamstresses, who taught me how to drape fabric, draft a pattern, and even alter any item of clothing to fit in the most flattering ways. The results of their efforts were always amazing. I'm certain their influence not only was a very strong part of me being awarded Fashion Trendsetter honors, but also manifests itself in my love of designing my own line of products which I create for women to enjoy.

Making matching Christmas pajamas is a tradition that continues, but now all the kids get to vote on the fabric and theme. Last year was flamingoes for my show in Vegas.

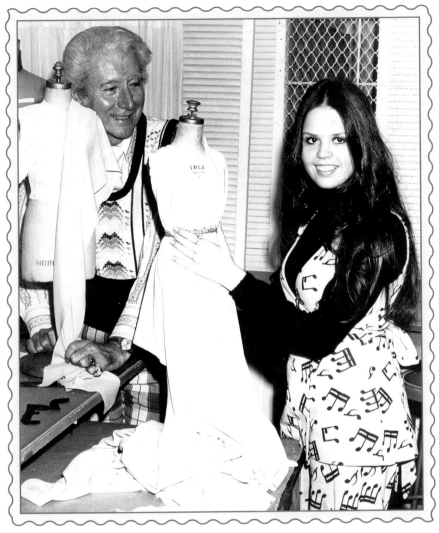

I could always be found in the studio wardrobe department taking notes from the pros. And *wearing* notes, too, for some reason! Fashion don't!

My daughter Brianna made me this jewelry box as a gift. Its value to me is priceless!

This sweet card my youngest made for me is far more precious than any gold record.

It's an incredible feeling to know that something has been handmade just for you, but it doesn't have to be a show-stopping gown. I still have hand-drawn birthday cards from my kids and friends that I've cherished for years. (Being a mom of eight, once in a while I'll find something that I didn't realize I had held onto for years, like a half-eaten cheese stick that has become a petrified relic in the back of a kitchen drawer! Not pleasant!)

One recent Christmas, my 12-year-old daughter made me a jewelry box with hand-painted designs on the outside and a velvet fabric lining. It's more precious to me than any amount of jewelry I could put in it. I don't keep my career "awards" in my house. I keep them in my office. I keep only my life "rewards" in my home. These are the handmade items created with love (and precious time) by my children and friends.

Obviously, there is an endless supply of potential gifts in stores and online that might be considered hip, trendy, and desirable. But I really do believe that handmade gifts are the best way to tell the ones you love that they are worth your effort and worth your time. With a handmade gift you can give the receiver the amazing experience of having something that is one-of-a-kind and personalized to their distinct style. Best of all, you'll be surprised how easy it is to do.

For this, my first craft book, I chose a variety of projects that would make great gifts for almost every occasion. You can make them for yourself, too! There's no harm in a trial run, or as we say in show business, "a good dress rehearsal." I selected handmade gifts that fit many lifestyles, from new mothers, to pet owners, and even those who love to bake. There are also some projects included that can be made with or for a teenager, and great ideas for your own home decor.

The instructions are easy to follow, like a favorite recipe, and the photos are included as an example of the finished gift. My hope is that, just like when cooking, you will experience the fun of expressing your own creative style by trying out varied techniques and "ingredients" to make every project to your exact taste.

At this point in my life, I only want to work on projects, both professionally and personally, that have meaning and bring joy to others. I've been in the finest hotels, palaces, and multimillion-dollar homes—all filled with the best luxury items available. However, I can sincerely say that most of those places, though beautiful, lack that personalization made from a loving heart. I've also been in modest, small homes bursting with a welcoming feeling and the luxury of handmade comforts like quilts, pillows, and picture frames filled with photos of family and friends. I'd rather fill my heart up there, any day.

I'm delighted by the apparent resurgence of women and even men who are interested in sewing, knitting, embroidery, and crafting of all types. When I was a child, many households had sewing machines, but this seemed to decline as more women went into the work force. These days, we might be looking for a little piece of "home" again. Maybe we've even come full circle as the sale of sewing machines has increased rapidly in the past few years. I'd love to think that the next generation could experience the joy and feeling of accomplishment that sewing, quilting, and crafting can give. In my own home, you can often find my kids, their friends, and my friends gathered in the room where I keep my sewing machine and craft cabinet full of supplies. It is there that we have our most heartfelt discussions. Busy hands are a great way to have fun and catch up on what's going on in each other's lives . . . and it's great therapy!

On the wall in my crafting room I've hung a quilt, made by hand and dedicated to my mother, that will be a gift passed to my children. In 2006, I decided that a quilt that could become an heirloom was a perfect way to honor my mother's life. I gathered together the various keepsakes that had not suffered damage in the house fire and designed each block to feature one aspect of her life that she loved most. I started with the very last cross-stitch she was working on, which I left in the hoop with the needle still tucked into the design, right where she had left it, unfinished. In another square I attached the actual pearls she wore on her wedding day, arranging them around the marriage photo of her and my dad. Try doing that in a scrapbook! Another

A quilt made as a tribute to my mother that I know she would have treasured. She taught me to love sewing and quilting and the powerful memories that can be created for generations to come.

saxophone, and now my youngest son, Matthew, has taken it up so he can play "like Grandma did."

One square displays my mom's love of genealogy, and another her dedication to cooking for her husband and children. Every square emphasizes her love of the life God gave her and illustrates where my mother placed her priorities.

Even my first-grader, Abigail "Olive-May" (she was named after her grandma), who is too young to remember my mother, loves to look at the quilt and hear the stories of her grandma's life. By the way, she and I just picked out fabrics so that we can make a quilt for her dolls, together. I know my mother would absolutely love to see those traditions continue.

I hope that, like me, you fall in love with making handmade gifts. I believe we should treat our creativity in the way that my mother did: like a lavish gift that can bring happiness to others and the joy of service into our own lives. It's always those gifts we make and give with all our heart that, in return, are a blessing to our souls.

Enjoy! I can't wait to see what you make. Send pictures!!

Marie Osmond

square features a stitching of her scriptures and the name badge she wore as a missionary for our church, with charms identifying the various locations she and my father served. Embroidered on another square are the lyrics from my mom's favorite song, which my family sung in harmony to her on many occasions: "I wouldn't trade the silver in my mother's hair for all the gold in the world." In that square is an antique locket containing a snippet of her silver hair. She grew up playing the saxophone, so one was embroidered onto another square. She taught each of us to appreciate her love of the

GIFTS
for Mothers and Little Ones

Celebrating a new addition to the family by making a sweet
quilt, adorable outfit, or cute baby accessory is a gesture certain
to bring multiplied happiness, because the parents will love it,
too. Handmade personalized gifts can be as unique as each child
and may hold memories for a lifetime. The ideas on these pages
will transform even the most practical baby necessity into a
meaningful gift that any Mommy will appreciate. It doesn't get
any more fun than sewing for a child!

My First Doll Quilt

The first project I chose for this book is in honor of my quilting debut as a very little girl, a Nine Patch doll quilt my mother made with me (see page 7). I'm sure I was a big help! In this replica, I continued the original theme by using a wide variety of '30s reproduction prints combined with solid-colored fabrics. These days I make doll quilts with my own daughters. It's a fun way to give a first-time quilter a great sense of accomplishment. This quilt is even the perfect size for a newborn.

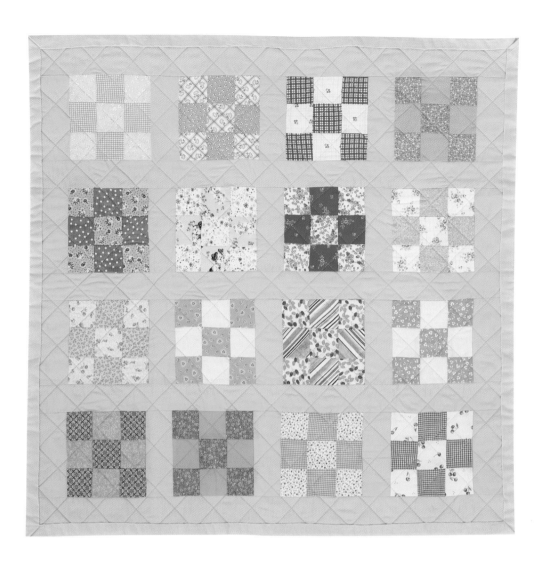

SERVING SIZE

1 quilt, 34" x 34"

16 blocks, 6" x 6"

INGREDIENTS

¾ yard of pink solid for sashing and borders

32 assorted scraps, at least 2½" x 10" each

1¼ yards of aqua solid for combined backing and binding

36" x 36" piece of batting

PREP WORK

From the pink solid, cut:

9 strips, 2½" x 42"; crosscut into:

    5 strips, 2½" x 34½"

    20 rectangles, 2½" x 6½"

From each of 16 of the assorted scraps, cut:

5 squares, 2½" x 2½"

From each of the remaining 16 scraps, cut:

4 squares, 2½" x 2½"

From the aqua solid, cut:

1 rectangle, 38" x 38"

ASSEMBLING THE QUILT

1. For each block, select five 2½" squares of one fabric and four 2½" squares of a contrasting fabric. Lay out the squares in a Nine Patch block formation as shown. Sew the squares into three rows of three squares each, and then sew the rows together. Make 16 blocks (fig. A). Press.

2. Arrange the completed blocks in four rows of four blocks each. Place a 2½" x 6½" pink rectangle between the blocks in each row. Sew the blocks and strips together to form the four rows. Add a 2½" x 6½" pink rectangle to each end of the rows (fig. B). Press all seam allowances toward the pink strips.

3. Sew a 2½" x 34½" pink strip to the bottom of each row. Press the seam allowances toward the pink strips. Then sew the rows together in your desired order, always with the pink strip on the bottom. When the rows are all assembled, add the remaining pink strip to the top of your quilt (fig. C).

FINISHING THE QUILT

1. Layer the backing fabric right side down on your worktable. Center the batting square on top of it, smoothing out any wrinkles. Place the quilt top right side up on top of the layers, again taking care to center it. Pin the layers together or baste them with thread.

2. The quilt shown was machine quilted in an allover crosshatch pattern—diagonal lines that run through the squares in the quilt blocks and continue through the sashing strips. This is an easy way to finish a Nine Patch quilt and the machine quilting will hold up to the multiple washings that this doll quilt is bound to require!

3. Using scissors, carefully trim the excess batting even with the edges of the quilt top. Take care not to cut through the backing fabric.

4. Fold the excess backing fabric to the front of the quilt, bringing the raw edge of the fabric even with the edge of the quilt top. Fold again, this time bringing the folded edge to overlap the quilt top edges by ¼". Fold the corners to form miters as shown (fig. D).

5. Pin the folded fabric edge in place, and then stitch by hand or machine to secure.

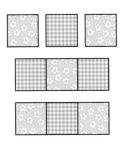
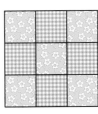

Nine Patch block.
Make 16.

Fig. A

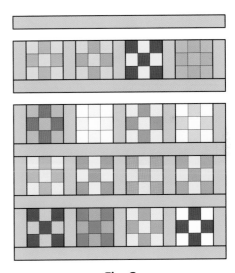

Fig. C

Make 4 rows.

Fig. B

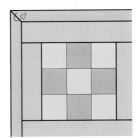

Fig. D

This is my youngest child's cherished quilt. It's her favorite because all of the flying friends quilted into its cheery design: the dragonfly, bee, butterfly, and bird, which symbolize new beginnings, purity, strength, and happiness. The springtime flowers feature ribbon and rickrack stems, and can be personalized with embroidery, buttons, lace, or whatever you choose. On Abigail's quilt are embroidered lyrics from a song about adoption that I've performed on stage: "From God's Arms, to My Arms, to Yours," because my heart tells me that she arrived on the wings of angels.

My Favorite Things Baby Quilt

SERVING SIZE

1 quilt, 49" x 63"

INGREDIENTS

Yardage is based on 42"-wide fabric unless otherwise noted. A fat quarter measures approximately 18" x 21".

1 fat quarter each of pink print, pink checked fabric, mauve print, mauve solid, tan print, beige solid, tan solid, dark brown print, and 3 green prints for patchwork and appliqués

1 yard of medium green print for patchwork blocks and outer border

1 yard of brown-and-rose print for appliqué, patchwork, inner border, and binding

1 fat quarter of peach print for appliqué background and patchwork

1 fat quarter of mint green print for appliqué background and patchwork

1 fat quarter of cream print for appliqué background and patchwork

1 fat quarter of light pink print for appliqué background and patchwork

3 yards of backing fabric

54" x 68" piece of batting

2 yards of 17"-wide fusible web

Dark brown embroidery floss

½ yard of ½"-wide green velvet ribbon

⅓ yard of ⅛"-wide picot-edged green satin ribbon

⅓ yard of ⅜"-wide green sheer ribbon

¼ yard of ¼"-wide green velvet ribbon

¼ yard of narrow green rickrack

PREP WORK

To make the best use of your fabrics, make sure to cut the pieces in the order listed below. Then use all of the remaining fabrics as desired for the various patchwork blocks. (Cutting dimensions are given with each set of block instructions.) Cut the appliqué shapes last.

From the peach print, cut:
1 rectangle, 13½" x 20½"

From the cream print, cut:
1 strip, 8½" x 42"; crosscut into:
   2 rectangles, 8½" x 10½"
   1 square, 8½" x 8½"

From the light pink print, cut:
1 square, 8½" x 8½"

From the tan print, cut:
1 square, 6½" x 6½"

From the pink checked fabric, cut:
1 square, 6½" x 6½"
2 strips, 1½" x 8½"

From the mint green print, cut:
1 square, 8½" x 8½"
1 rectangle, 4½" x 5½"
1 rectangle, 3½" x 4½"

From the brown-and-rose print, cut:
5 strips, 1½" x 42"
6 strips, 2½" x 42"
1 square, 8½" x 8½"

From the medium green print, cut:
6 strips, 5" x 42"

PATCHWORK BLOCKS

The quilt shown has a scrappy feel, so the following instructions tell you the sizes and number of pieces to cut, but you can choose which fabrics you'd like to use for each block. Use ¼"-wide seam allowances throughout.

Pinwheel Blocks (Make 12)

1. Cut 12 pairs of 4" x 4" light squares (24 total) and 12 pairs of 4" x 4" medium squares (24 total). Each block uses two matching light squares and two matching medium squares.

2. Using a pencil and ruler, draw a diagonal line from corner to corner on the wrong side of each light square. Lay a light square right sides together with a medium square. Repeat with the matching squares. Stitch ¼" from each side of the drawn line. Cut the squares apart on the drawn line and press the resulting four matching triangle squares open. Repeat with all pairs of squares to make 12 sets of four matching triangle squares. Trim the triangle squares to measure 3½" square (fig. A).

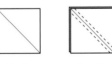

Mark.   Stitch.   Cut.

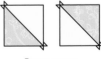

Press open.

Fig. A

3. Sew the matching triangle squares together as shown to make 12 Pinwheel blocks (fig. B). Your blocks should measure 6½" square.

Triangle Square Blocks (Make Seven)

1. Cut four light and four medium or dark 5" x 5" squares. Choose the fabrics randomly or as desired.

2. Draw a diagonal line on the wrong side of the light squares as in step 2 of the Pinwheel blocks on page 17.

3. Place each light square on a medium or dark square, right sides together. Stitch ¼" from each side of the line as for the Pinwheel blocks. Cut and press as before.

4. Trim the resulting triangle squares to 4½" square. You'll have eight Triangle Square blocks; one will be extra (fig. C).

Square-in-a-Square Blocks (Make Five)

1. In the quilt shown, some of these blocks have light center squares while others have dark centers. Select fabrics as desired. For each block, cut:

   One center square, 4¾" x 4¾" (five total)

   Two contrasting squares, 3⅞" x 3⅞"; cut the squares in half diagonally to yield 20 triangles (five pairs of four matching triangles)

2. Select one square and four matching triangles. Carefully fold the triangles in half and crease to mark the midpoint of the long edge.

3. Position one triangle, right sides together, along one side of the square, and then stitch. Repeat, stitching another triangle to the

opposite side of the square. Press the triangles open and away from the center square (fig. D).

4. In the same manner, sew the two remaining triangles to the other sides of the square. Press. Repeat to make five blocks (fig. E). The finished blocks should measure 6½" square.

Nine Patch Blocks (Make Four)

1. Select two contrasting fabrics for each Nine Patch block. You'll need five squares of one fabric and four of the other for each block. Cut all squares 2½" x 2½".

2. Lay out the squares in three rows of three squares each, alternating the two colors. Sew the squares together in rows and press the seam allowances toward the darker fabric. Sew the rows together and press. Repeat to make four blocks (fig. F). They should measure 6½" square.

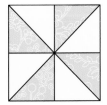

Pinwheel block.
Make 12.

Fig. B

Triangle square.
Make 7.

Fig. C

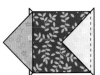

Fig. D

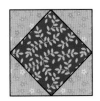

Square-in-a-Square block.
Make 5.

Fig. E

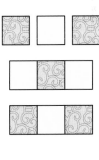

Nine Patch block.
Make 4.

Fig. F

Four Patch Blocks
(Make Two Large and One Small)

1. Choose two fabrics for each block. For the large blocks, cut two squares, 3" x 3", of each fabric. For the small block, cut two squares, 2" x 2", from each fabric.

2. Lay out the squares for each block so like fabrics are in opposite corners. Sew the pairs of squares together in a row, and then sew the rows together. Large blocks should measure 5½" square and the small block should measure 3½" square (fig. G).

Flying Geese Blocks (Make 22)

1. The Flying Geese blocks are stitched together in two strips in this quilt. They're very scrappy, using just about all the fabrics in the quilt. For each unit you'll need two fabrics, a medium or dark fabric for the large center "goose" and a lighter background fabric. From assorted fabrics, cut 22 rectangles, 2" x 3½", for the geese. From contrasting fabrics, cut 22 pairs of squares (44 total), 2" x 2".

2. Draw a diagonal line from corner to corner on the wrong side of each light square, as for the Pinwheel blocks on page 17.

3. Place a light square, right sides together, on a dark rectangle. Stitch on the drawn line, and then cut away the excess corner fabric, leaving a ¼" seam allowance. Repeat, stitching a matching light square on the opposite end of the rectangle (fig. H).

4. Repeat to make 22 Flying Geese blocks. Stitch the blocks together in two strips, one with 12 geese and one with 10. The finished strips should measure 3½" x 18½" and 3½" x 15½" (fig. I).

Filler Squares

1. The fun arrangement of the blocks in this quilt makes it interesting to look at, but also requires a few extra squares here and there to fill in the gaps between the blocks. From assorted fabrics, cut a total of 21 squares, 2½" x 2½".

2. Sew one strip of 10 squares side by side, one strip of 3 squares side by side, and then one short strip of 2 squares side by side (fig. J).

3. Sew the remaining six squares together in a two-by-three arrangement (fig. K).

MAKING THE APPLIQUÉ BLOCKS

The appliqué patterns are on foldout pattern page 1 at the back of the book. Prepare the shapes for fusible appliqué by tracing the pattern onto fusible web, and then ironing the web to the wrong side of your selected fabrics. Cut out the pieces on the drawn lines.

In the quilt shown, the appliqués are fused in place, and then blanket-stitched with dark brown thread to secure the edges. Feel free to use your favorite appliqué method. If you use needle-turn or freezer-paper appliqué you'll need to add seam allowances when cutting out the fabrics.

Four Patch blocks.
Make 2 large and 1 small.

Fig. G

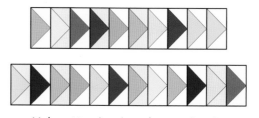

Make a 10-unit strip and a 12-unit strip.

Fig. I

Make 1.

Fig. K

Flying Geese unit

Fig. H

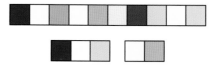

Make 1 of each.

Fig. J

Flower Block

1. Using the 13½" x 20½" peach print rectangle for the block background, refer to the quilt photo on page 18 for flower placement ideas. Fuse the flower and leaf appliqués in place and blanket-stitch around each. Position the various ribbons as desired for stems and machine stitch them in place.

2. Add hand- or machine-embroidery details as desired. Here, my daughter Abigail's name along with her birth date, birth weight, and length were hand embroidered using an outline stitch (fig. L).

Birdhouse Block

1. Using one of the 8½" x 10½" cream rectangles for the background, appliqué the birdhouse, center hole, and roof in place. After they're complete, add the flower details at the bottom-left corner.

2. Sew the 1½" x 8½" pink checked strips to the top and bottom of the block. Press the seam allowances toward the strips.

Butterfly Block

1. Using the 8½" light pink square for the background, appliqué the butterfly wings onto the block. Appliqué the large and small circles and the butterfly body on top.

2. Add embroidery details as desired. In my quilt, the antennae and a swirl have been embroidered using an outline stitch.

Bumblebee Block

1. Using the 6½" tan print square for the background, appliqué the bumblebee body in place. Add the head, stripes, and finally the wings on top.

2. Embroider the antennae and a swirl using an outline stitch.

Heart-in-Hand Block

1. Using the 6½" pink checked square for the background, appliqué the hand onto the square. Add the heart on top.

2. Add the embroidered message, if desired, making sure to keep the words well away from the seam allowance area. My message reads: "From God's arms to your arms to mine." Customize the message if you'd like.

Dragonfly Block

1. Using the 8½" mint green square for the background, appliqué the dragonfly body and wings in place, tucking the ends of the wings under the body.

2. Embroider the antennae in place. You'll want to wait until the quilt top is assembled to add the swirl at the tail end, because it travels over more than one block in the quilt.

Bird Block

1. Using the remaining 8½" x 10½" cream rectangle for the background, appliqué the bird in place. Add the wing and beak.

2. Embroider the legs using an outline stitch. Add the eyes using satin stitch (fig. M).

Baby Carriage Block

1. Using the 8½" brown-and-rose square for the background, appliqué the baby carriage and handle in place. Add the hood and wheels on top.

2. Embroider the lines in the carriage hood by hand or machine.

Heart Block

1. Using the 8½" cream square for the background, appliqué the large heart in place.

2. Center the smaller heart on top of the large one and appliqué in place.

Outline stitch

Fig. L

Satin stitch

Fig. M

ASSEMBLING THE QUILT TOP

This quilt is assembled in sections, which at first looks a bit tricky. But by using a partial seam technique, no set-in seams are needed and you'll find this puzzle-style quilt is quite fun to put together. Believe me, it's much easier (and more fun) to sew together than it is to explain! Be sure to press the seam allowances as you go.

Section 1: Bottom of Quilt

1. Starting at the bottom-right corner, sew together a Nine Patch, a Pinwheel, and two Square-in-a-Square blocks for row 1 (fig. N).

2. For row 2, sew the Bird block to the left of the Baby Carriage block. Then sew the two-square unit to the top of a Pinwheel block, aligning the squares to the top right edge of the Pinwheel. Notice that the square unit isn't as long as the Pinwheel. That's OK; just don't sew the entire seam. Start stitching at the outer edge and sew for about 3". Backstitch and cut the threads. This is the first partial seam. Sew this Pinwheel unit to the left of the Bird block (fig. O). Then join row 2 to the top of row 1.

3. For row 3 of the section, sew together a Pinwheel, a Nine Patch, a Pinwheel, and the six-square unit. Sew this row to the top of

the unit from step 2. Then add the Dragonfly block to the left end of the row. Notice that you can easily sew a complete seam because the two-square unit at the bottom of the row hasn't been fully attached (fig. P).

4. For row 4, sew together from left to right a Pinwheel, the Bumblebee block, another Pinwheel, the Hand block, and a third Pinwheel (fig. Q). Join this row to the top of the Dragonfly row.

5. Sew the two large Four Patch blocks together to make a vertical row 5. Add the 4½" x 5½" mint green rectangle to the bottom of the row (fig. R). Join this row to the left side of the assembled piece.

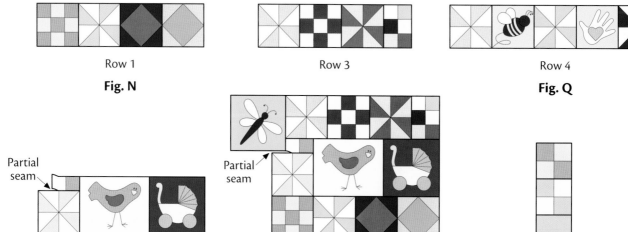

Row 1
Fig. N

Row 3

Row 4
Fig. Q

Row 2
Fig. O

Fig. P

Partial seam

Partial seam

Row 5
Fig. R

6. Join the three-square strip to the top of a Square-in-a-Square block. Then sew this combined unit to the left of the Heart block (fig. S).

7. Sew two Triangle Square blocks together side by side. Add the 3½" x 4½" mint green rectangle to the left end of this row. Sew this row to the top of the Heart row, aligning the raw edges on the right end and sewing a partial seam. Leave the last 2" or 3" of the seam unsewn (fig. T).

8. Sew the section from step 7 to the bottom-left edge of the main section. Now go back to the partial seam by the Dragonfly block and complete that seam, sewing the Dragonfly block to the two Triangle Square blocks (fig. U). Wasn't that easy?

9. Sew the 12-unit Flying Geese strip to the left edge of your large unit, adjoining it to the large Four Patches and mint green rectangles. Now go back and complete the partial seam to complete the bottom half of the quilt top (fig. V).

Section 2: Top of Quilt

1. For the left portion, sew a Square-in-a-Square block, two Pinwheel blocks, and a Nine Patch block into a vertical row (fig. W).

2. For the center portion, sew two Pinwheel blocks together, and then add a Nine Patch to the left of the Pinwheels. Sew the small Four Patch block to the end of the 10-unit Flying Geese strip. Sew this row to the bottom of the Pinwheel row (fig. X).

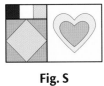

Fig. S

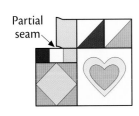

Partial seam

Fig. T

Complete seam.

Fig. U

Fig. W

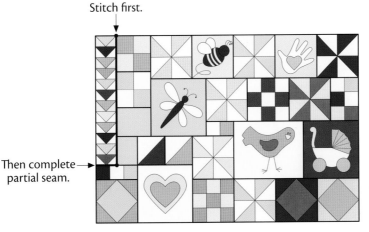

Stitch first.

Then complete partial seam.

Fig. V

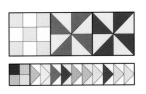

Join rows.

Fig. X

3. Sew the 10-square strip to the bottom of the Flower block. Then sew this unit to the bottom of the Flying Geese unit from step 2. Notice that the Flower block is longer than the Flying Geese. Be sure to align both units along the left raw edges (fig. Y). This "gap" will be covered by the Birdhouse block.

4. Sew the remaining Pinwheel and Square-in-a-Square blocks together. Join this unit to the right edge of the Birdhouse block (fig. Z).

5. Sew the remaining Triangle Square blocks together in a three-block horizontal row and a two-block vertical row. Sew the two-block row to the left of the Butterfly block. Then join the three-block strip to the top of this unit (fig. AA).

6. Join the Birdhouse unit to the top of the Butterfly unit, aligning the rows at the right-hand edge. Sew the seam, leaving the last 1" or so unsewn (fig. BB).

7. Join the Butterfly unit to the Flower unit, aligning the pieces at the bottom edge. Sew the seam all the way to the end of the Triangle Square blocks. Then fold the Birdhouse block right sides together with the Pinwheel block in the top row. Sew this seam as far as you can, stopping about 1" from the bottom of the Flying Geese unit.

Complete the top half of the quilt by turning under the edges at the bottom-left corner of the Birdhouse block and hand stitching them in place to the corner of the Flower block (fig. CC).

8. Join the top of the quilt to the bottom of the quilt!

ADDING THE BORDERS

1. Measure the length of your quilt top. (It should be 52½".) Sew three of the brown-and-rose 1½"-wide strips together end to end, and then from this long strip, cut two lengths the same length as your quilt top. Sew these strips to the sides of your quilt top. Press the seam allowances toward the borders.

Fig. Y

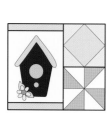

Fig. Z

Fig. AA

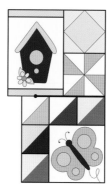

Sew seam from right edge to dot.

Fig. BB

Turn under seam allowance at corner of block and slipstitch in place.

Fig. CC

2. Measure the width of your quilt top, including the brown borders. (It should be 40½".) Trim the remaining two 1½"-wide brown-and-rose strips to this width and sew them to the top and bottom of the quilt top.

3. Add the outer green borders in the same manner, measuring the quilt, piecing the strips, and trimming them to fit. Add the side borders first, followed by the top and bottom borders.

FINISHING DETAILS

1. Add any final embroidery details, including the swirl on the Dragonfly block and adjacent mint green patches.

2. Layer and baste the quilt top, batting, and backing and machine quilt as desired. Or take your project to your favorite long-arm quilter for quilting.

3. Join the 2½"-wide brown-and-rose strips end to end to make binding. Attach the binding to the quilt.

This is the diaper bag that had all my girlfriends oohing and aahing. It can carry all the essentials: diapers, wipes, pacifiers, toys, and the all-important cell phone! Believe me, after twenty years and eight babies in diapers, I know a good bag! This one has a place for everything and even includes a coordinating changing mat, which is an appreciated extra that's simple to make. I made sure that this diaper bag closes with a zipper because the contents need to stay put no matter how many times baby tips the whole thing over.

Thoroughly Modern Diaper Bag

SERVING SIZE

1 zippered diaper bag, 16" x 14½", with pockets inside and out

1 padded changing mat, 12" x 24"

INGREDIENTS

Yardage is based on 42"-wide fabric unless otherwise noted.

2 yards of medium green print for bag top, sides, and bottom; bag lining; handles; patchwork; and changing-mat cover

1½ yards of pink checked fabric for exterior pocket, interior pockets, bias binding, appliqué, and patchwork

⅜ yard of mint green print for exterior pocket, binding, and patchwork

Fat quarter of green checked fabric for inside back pocket

Fat quarters or scraps of assorted brown, green, pink, cream, and tan prints for patchwork and appliqué; sort scraps by light and medium/dark values

1⅛ yards of 45"-wide batting

7" and 16" zippers

½ yard of ¼"- or ⅜"-wide elastic

1⅝ yards of 2"-wide waistband interfacing for handles

1 purchased waterproof changing pad, approximately 12" x 24"

1 covered button, ⅝" diameter

Brown embroidery floss or pearl cotton

PREP WORK

Cutting information for the main pieces of the diaper bag and changing mat are listed below. Cut all of these pieces first. Then use the leftovers along with the other scrap fabrics to cut the pieces needed for the Flying Geese, Four Patches, and the fusible appliqués.

From the medium green print and referring to figure A, cut *on the lengthwise grain:*

2 strips, 7½" x 44", for the bag and lining sides/bottom

2 strips, 4½" x 28½", for bag handles

From the remaining medium green print and referring to figure A, cut:

2 rectangles, 14" x 17", for front and back lining

2 pieces, 8" x 18½", for outer side pockets

2 pieces, 7" x 16½", for bag top

4 pieces, 3¾" x 14", for bag front and back

2 strips, 2¼" x 8", for side-pocket binding

1 rectangle, 11½" x 23½", for changing-mat cover

Save scraps for patchwork units.

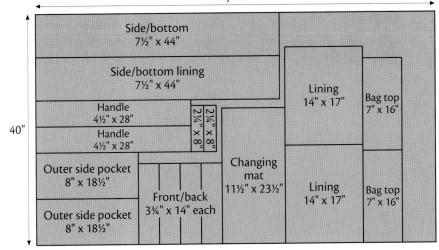

Cutting for diaper bag

Fig. A

From ½ *yard of the pink checked fabric, cut:*

1 rectangle, 16" x 17", for interior pocket

1 rectangle, 8" x 17", for exterior-pocket lining

1 rectangle, 8" x 11", for bird pocket

1 square, 7½" x 7½", for zippered pocket

1 rectangle, 2½" x 7½", for zippered pocket

Save scraps for appliqués and patchwork.

From the remaining 1 yard of pink checked fabric, cut *on the bias:*

240" total of 2¼"-wide strips for bias binding

From the mint green print, cut:

1 rectangle, 8" x 17", for exterior-pocket lining

1 rectangle, 8" x 11", for butterfly pocket

1 strip, 2¼" x 17", for pocket binding

From the green checked fabric, cut:

1 rectangle, 13" x 17", for inside-back pocket

From the assorted light scraps, cut:

56 pairs of matching squares, 2" x 2" (112 total)

14 squares, 2½" x 2½"

From the assorted medium/dark scraps, cut:

56 rectangles, 2" x 3½"

14 squares, 2½" x 2½"

From the batting, cut:

2 rectangles, 18" x 20"

1 rectangle, 9" x 36"

2 rectangles, 14" x 17"

2 rectangles, 8" x 17"

2 rectangles, 8" x 9"

2 strips, 7½" x 44"

ASSEMBLING THE BAG SECTIONS

The front, back, and side/bottom sections are each assembled independently and machine quilted before the overall bag is assembled. The quilted layers give the bag stability.

Bag Front and Back

1. Make a total of 56 Flying Geese units, referring to "Flying Geese Blocks" on page 20 and using the medium/dark 2" x 3½" rectangles and pairs of light 2" squares. Sew the geese together in four strips of nine geese each and four strips of five geese each (fig. B).

2. Using the light and medium/dark 2½" squares, make two checkerboard strips that are two squares wide and seven squares long, alternating the color values (fig. C).

3. Sew medium green 3¾"-wide strips to each side of both checkerboard strips. Sew nine-unit strips of Flying Geese to opposite sides of the green strips. Note that the checkerboard strips are a bit longer than the other strips. Align all strips at the top edge and trim the bottom of the checkerboard after assembling the bag front and back. Press the seam allowances toward the green strips. The finished pieces should measure 14" x 17" (fig. D).

4. Lay one of the green print 14" x 17" rectangles right side down; layer on top of it a 14" x 17" batting rectangle and one of the pieced sections from step 3. Pin or baste the layers together and machine quilt as desired. Repeat to make two. Trim the quilted pieces to 16" x 14½".

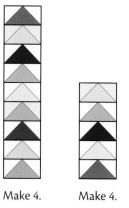

Make 4. Make 4.

Fig. B

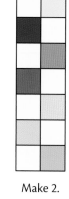

Make 2.

Fig. C

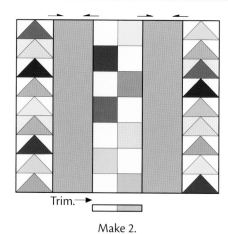

Trim.→

Make 2.

Fig. D

Inside Pockets

This bag has three interior pockets. Along the back side, there is a zippered pocket to securely hold car keys, a cell phone, or other small items you don't want to lose in the bottom of the bag. There is also a long pocket that is stitched in two places to create three open compartments. Along the inside front is one long open pocket for stashing the changing mat.

1. For the divided inside-back pocket, fold the green checked 13" x 17" rectangle in half, *wrong* sides together, to create a 6½" x 17" rectangle. Press.

2. Place the pocket on the lining side of the bag back, aligning the raw edges at the bottom. Baste in place along the side and bottom edges.

3. To divide the pocket into three sections, machine stitch from the bag front, sewing in the ditch along the checkerboard seam lines (fig. E).

4. For the zippered pocket, fold the pink checked 2½" x 7½" rectangle

in half lengthwise, right sides together. Stitch the short ends with a ¼" seam allowance, and then turn right side out and press. Repeat for the pink checked 7½" square. Turn right side out and press.

5. Align the folded edge of the smaller rectangle to one edge of the zipper teeth on the 7" zipper. Edgestitch in place, and then topstitch ¼" from the edge stitching (fig. F).

6. Fold under ½" along the raw edge of the larger rectangle. Align this edge to the other edge of the zipper teeth, making sure the ends of both pocket pieces are also aligned. Stitch the pocket piece to the zipper tape in the same manner (fig.G).

7. Center the finished pocket along the top inside edge of the bag back (the raw edge of the pocket should be flush with the raw edge of the bag back) and edgestitch in place.

8. For the changing-mat pocket, fold and press the pink checked

16" x 17" rectangle in half, *wrong* sides together, to make an 8" x 17" rectangle. Align the raw edges of the rectangle with the lower and side edges of the inside bag front and machine baste in place.

Outside Pockets

1. To make the outside front and back pockets, prepare the bird and butterfly appliqués (patterns are on foldout pattern page 1) for fusible appliqué. Appliqué the butterfly onto the mint green 8" x 11" rectangle and the bird onto the pink checked 8" x 11" rectangle. Sew a five-unit Flying Geese strip to each short end of the rectangles. Press (fig. H).

2. Lay the mint green and pink checked 8" x 17" rectangles right side down on your table. Place a piece of same-size batting on top of each. Then place the assembled pocket on top of each, with the appliqué background matching the pocket lining fabric. Machine baste around the perimeter of each.

Stitch along vertical seam lines to make 3 pocket openings.

Fig. E

Fig. F

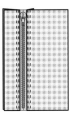

Fig. G

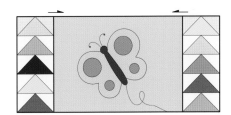

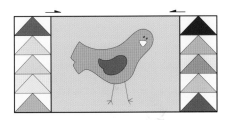

Fig. H

3. Fold the mint green 2¼" x 17" strip in half, right sides together, to make double-fold binding. Sew it to the top edge of the green pocket using a ¼" seam allowance. Fold the binding over the top of the pocket and hand stitch on the inside edge to secure. Bind the pink pocket in the same manner, cutting a 17"-long strip from your pink checked bias strips.

4. Pin a pocket to the front and the back of the bag, aligning the raw edge at the bottom of the bag. Machine baste in place along the side and bottom edges (fig. I).

Bag Sides and Bottom

1. Layer the two medium green 7½" x 44" strips, right sides out, with a layer of batting in between. Machine quilt the layers together as desired to add strength to the bag bottom. Trim the batting even with the green fabric.

2. Lay an 8" x 9" piece of batting on the wrong side of each medium green 8" x 18½" rectangle, with the batting even with one end of the strip. Fold the strip over the batting, so the right side of the fabric is showing on both sides of the batting (fig. J). Machine quilt as desired.

3. Position the quilted pockets on the 44"-long quilted strip so that the folded edge of the pockets is 11" from the ends of the strip and the raw edges of the pockets are facing toward the center of the strip as shown (fig. K). Machine stitch along the folded edge of the pockets through all layers to secure the pocket bottoms to the bag sides.

4. Bind the top edge of each pocket using the medium green 2¼" x 8" strips. Leave the outer edges open so that the binding forms a casing. Using a safety pin, thread elastic through the finished casing and draw up to 7". Machine baste the ends of the elastic, stitching in the seam allowance, to secure (fig. L).

5. Flip the pocket away from the center of the bag bottom and baste the side edges in place.

Bag Top

1. Fold each medium green 7" x 16½" rectangle in half lengthwise with *wrong* sides together and press.

2. Insert the 16" zipper as for the small zippered pocket on page 29, centering the zipper so that you have a ¼" seam allowance at each end of the zipper.

BAG ASSEMBLY

1. Using a saucer or plastic lid, mark a gentle curve on each bottom corner of the front and back bag pieces. Trim along the marked lines.

2. Matching the bottom center of the bag front to the center of the side/ bottom strip, pin the pieces with lining sides together. Sew with a ⅜" seam allowance (fig. M). The seam and raw edges will be showing on the *outside* of the bag.

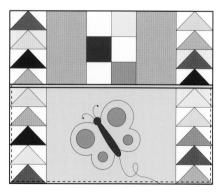

Machine baste pocket to bag.

Fig. I

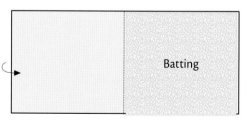

Fold in half.

Fig. J

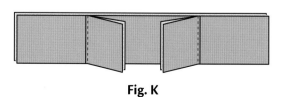

Fig. K

Batting

Fig. L

Sew the bag back to the side/bottom strip in the same manner.

3. Sew the bag top (with zipper opened) to the bag, matching the corners and using a ⅜" seam allowance.

Binding

1. Sew the pink checked 2¼" binding strips to the bag front and to the bag back along the previous stitching lines. Fold the binding over the raw edges to encase the seam allowances and stitch in place by hand or machine. Trim the binding ends even with the top of the bag.

2. Sew binding to the top of the bag along the seam line in the same manner.

Handles

1. Cut two 28" lengths of waistband interfacing.

2. Press under ¼" along one long edge of both of the medium green 4½" x 28½" strips.

3. Lay the interfacing on the wrong side of each strip, aligning it with the long edge that isn't pressed

under; machine baste in place. Tuck the raw edges of the fabric in toward the interfacing on each end of the handles. Press.

4. Wrap the fabric around the interfacing and stitch in place. Edgestitch along both sides of each handle, then topstitch ¼" from the edge stitching (fig. N).

5. Position the handles on the bag 2½" from the top edge and with the inside edge of the handle aligned with the seam line between the Flying Geese and the green strips. Stitch in place to secure, making sure the handles aren't twisted (fig. O).

CHANGING MAT

This handy changing mat (see the photo on page 20) couldn't be easier! Simply purchase a plastic changing pad, add a bit of fabric to one side, and attach coordinating binding for a high-end look.

1. Sew the remaining pink checked 2¼"-wide bias strips together end to end. Fold the long strip in half lengthwise, right sides together, and press.

2. Lay the green print 11½" x 23½" rectangle (or size to fit your changing pad) right side up on the changing pad. Machine baste close to the edge to secure. Trim the excess fabric from the curved corners.

3. Position the binding with the raw edges even with the outer edge of the changing pad. Stitch in place using a ¼" seam allowance. Fold the binding back on itself so that the folded edge covers the raw edge of the binding. Edgestitch in place.

4. If desired, use the petal pattern on pullout pattern page 1 to cut five pairs of petals. Sew the petal pairs right sides together, leaving the flat end open. Turn right side out and press. Machine baste across the bottom of the petals to gather. Stitch the petals to one end of the changing mat and cover the raw edges with a fabric-covered button. *Caution: Buttons are a choking hazard for babies, so you may want to attach with Velcro so that the flower decoration is removable.*

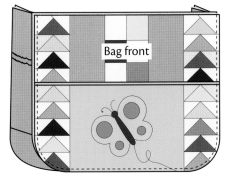

Stitch side/bottom strip to bag front with seam on outside of bag.

Fig. M

Fig. N

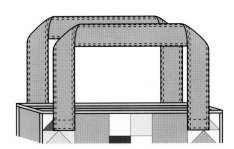

Topstitch handles in place.

Fig. O

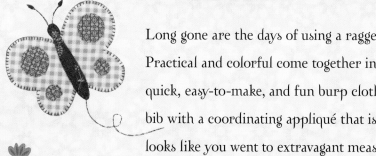

Long gone are the days of using a raggedy white diaper as a burp cloth! Practical and colorful come together in a very happy way with these really quick, easy-to-make, and fun burp cloths. You can even personalize a purchased bib with a coordinating appliqué that is charming, simple, and inexpensive, but looks like you went to extravagant measures. If you love the results as much as I do, you can make them to match the diaper bag on page 27.

make it tonight

Appliquéd Bib and Burp Cloths

SERVING SIZE

1 bib, 11½" x 15½", including tab closures

4 burp cloths, 13½" x 19½"

INGREDIENTS

Bib:

1 purchased stretch terry cloth bib with Velcro closure, approximately 9" x 12"

1 fat quarter of pink checked fabric for appliqué and binding

Scraps of brown and green prints for appliqué

6" scrap of fusible web

Brown thread for machine- or hand-embroidery details

Optional: 1 button to cover, ⅝" diameter

Burp Cloths:

6½" x 21½" piece *each* of 4 assorted pink, brown, and green prints for burp cloths (or 2 fat quarters)

20" x 24" piece of lightweight batting or fusible fleece

4 prefolded cloth diapers, approximately 13½" x 19½"

PREP WORK

Prepare the small butterfly body, wings, and dots for fusible appliqué using the patterns on pullout page 2.

From the pink checked fabric, cut: 100" of 2½"-wide bias strips

From the assorted pink, green, and brown prints, cut: 4 strips, 5½" x 20"

From the batting, cut: 4 strips, 5" x 19"

MAKING THE BIB

1. Following the manufacturer's instructions, prepare the butterfly body, wings, and dots for fusible appliqué. Position the pieces on the purchased bib, and then use a pressing cloth on top before fusing so that you don't scorch the terry fabric.

2. Blanket-stitch around the shapes by hand or machine. Add the antennae and swirl by machine or hand embroider it using an outline stitch (see page 21).

3. Sew the binding strips together end to end, and then press the strip in half lengthwise, right sides together. Starting along one straight edge, align the raw edges of the binding strip with the outer edges of the bib. Leave a 6" tail as you would for applying binding to a quilt and stitch the binding all the way around the bib, easing around the corners. Stop stitching about 6" from where you started. Trim the binding so that you have enough to overlap the starting tail by 2½".

4. Sew the two binding edges together with a diagonal seam, then refold the binding and stitch the loose bit to the bib.

5. Fold the binding over the raw edges of the bib and topstitch in place.

6. Optional: If desired, cover a button to coordinate with the bib and stitch in place over the tab closure. *Caution: Buttons are a choking hazard for small children, so you may want to substitute this with a fusible-appliqué circle for decoration.*

MAKING THE BURP CLOTHS

1. Press under ¼" on all edges of the pink, green, and brown 5½" x 20" strips.

2. Position a batting strip along the lengthwise center of each diaper. If you're using fusible fleece, press it in place to adhere, following the manufacturer's instructions.

3. Place a fabric strip right side up on top of each batting strip. Make sure the fabric completely covers the batting/fleece edges. Pin in place, and then edgestitch the fabric to the diaper (fig. A).

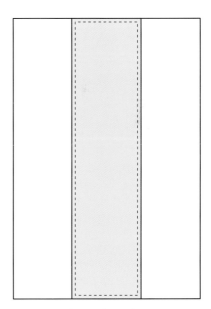

Edgestitch in place.

Fig. A

 This is the perfect last-minute gift when you don't have time to make a baby quilt from start to finish. You just need a couple of hours, a sweet cotton print, and a cozy fleece fabric to create this charming gift for Mom and Baby. My kids called these blankets their "softies" and couldn't sleep without them, so I think this project could almost come with a favorite "blankie" guarantee.

Oh-Sew-Easy Baby Blanket

SERVING SIZE

1 blanket, 30" x 39"

INGREDIENTS

1¼ yards of green floral print cotton fabric

1 yard of pink Minky Swirl or other fleece fabric

Optional: scraps of pink and green cotton fabrics and 4 buttons to cover, 1" diameter

PREP WORK

From the pink Minky, cut:
1 rectangle, 30" x 39"

From the green floral print, cut:
1 rectangle, 36" x 45"

From the pink and green cotton scraps, cut:
4 circles, 4¼" diameter, for optional yo-yos

ASSEMBLY

1. Press the green floral backing fabric to remove any wrinkles. Place right side down on your worktable. Fold over a 3"-wide border along each edge. Press the folds with your iron to crease the edges (fig. A).

2. To miter the corners of the cotton fabric, fold the excess fabric at the corners diagonally to form a miter and press the crease (fig. B). Repeat for all four corners.

3. Unfold the pressed miters and fold the fabric *right* sides together along the diagonal. Stitch the corners along the crease, stopping ¼" from the edge. Trim the excess fabric, leaving a ¼" seam allowance (fig. C).

4. When all four corners have been mitered, lay the green floral backing fabric on your worktable, right side down. Lay the pink Minky fabric right side up and centered on top of the backing fabric. Tuck the raw edges of the Minky fabric under the cotton fabric borders. Pin in place.

5. Turning under the raw edge of the border by ¼" as you go, topstitch the edge of the green floral cotton fabric, sewing through the border, the Minky, and the backing to secure (fig. D). Now wasn't that easy?

6. Optional Embellishments: To make the optional flower embellishments, make yo-yos using the 4¼" circles as follows. Fold under approximately ¼" around the edge of the circle and hand baste in place, taking smaller stitches on top and larger ones on bottom as you go. Pull the basting thread to gather the yo-yo. Flatten out the yo-yo and knot the thread. Sew one yo-yo in each corner of the blanket and add a fabric-covered button.

Caution: Buttons are a choking hazard for small children, so you may want to omit them and use just the yo-yos.

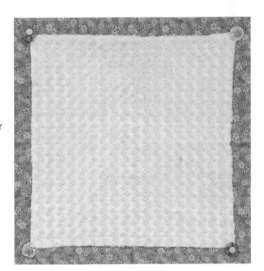

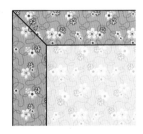

Fig. A

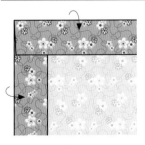

Fold excess fabric under on diagonal. Press.

Fig. B

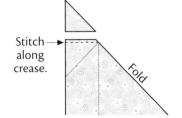

Stitch along crease.

Fig. C

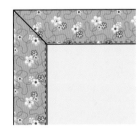

Edge stitch border to Minky.

Fig. D

Is this snuggy cute or what? I would have loved this as a gift when I first became a mommy. It's easy to bundle up Baby and be ready to go. Tuck tiny feet into the "pockets," and then wrap the two front pieces over Baby and secure with the Velcro tab. Choose a blue plush for a boy, or even have fun for baby's first Halloween by attaching little ears and a tail.

Baby Snuggy

SERVING SIZE

1 snuggy, 26" circumference when closed x 28" long, including hood and feet

INGREDIENTS

1 yard of pink smooth Minky

1 yard of pink plush Minky

⅝ yard of ⅛"-wide elastic

1 yard of 1½"-wide pink satin ribbon

2" square of Velcro fastener

Hand-sewing needle and pink thread

PREP WORK

The patterns for the snuggy pieces are on pullout pattern page 2.

From *both* the plush Minky and the smooth Minky, cut:

1 snuggy body (2 total)

1 hood (2 total)

2 feet (4 total)

ASSEMBLING THE SNUGGY

1. Sew the two hood pieces, right sides together, along the straight edge. Turn right side out.

2. Cut a 9" length of elastic. Place the elastic between the hood layers, about ¾" from the seam. Tack one end in place at the seam edge, and then, stretching the elastic as you go, stitch through both hood layers and elastic (fig. A).

3. Repeat steps 1 and 2 to make the two feet, this time using 5" lengths of elastic.

4. Lay the plush Minky body right side up on your worktable. Lay the feet and hood pieces on top, with the plush side facing the plush body. Machine baste in place. Then layer the smooth Minky body on top, right side facing the plush body piece. Pin in place, and then sew through all layers using a scant ½" seam allowance and leaving an opening along one long edge for turning (fig. B).

5. Clip the seam allowances at the sharp curve between the legs and turn right side out. Hand stitch the opening closed.

6. Wrap the left side over the right side to mark the positioning of the Velcro pieces. On the left side, stitch the Velcro on the underneath part of the wrap, and on the right side, stitch it on top.

7. Make a decorative ribbon rose by coiling the satin ribbon and hand stitching along one edge to secure it as you go. At first, coil tightly as for the center of a rose; then with each round, gather one edge of the ribbon more loosely until you've used the entire length of ribbon. Hand stitch in place over the Velcro stitching (fig. C).

Stitch elastic between layers.

Fig. A

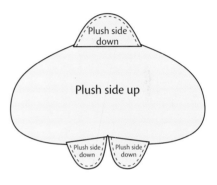

Plush side down

Plush side up

Plush side down   Plush side down

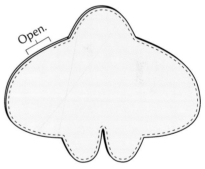

Open.

Leave open for turning.

Fig. B

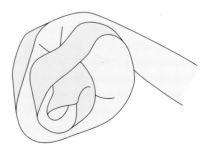

Fig. C

37

Here's my version of the original pillowcase dress, which was always a cute concept but too plain for my taste! I love a lot of color with some added fluff for little girl dresses: I've always been a "more is more" type when it comes to fun with fabric. The adorable bows on the shoulders and ruffled trim with a multidimensional flower on the pocket make this dress irresistible. It's detailed, but the steps for making it are simple to follow.

Easy-Peasy Little Girl's Dress

SERVING SIZE

1 dress, 21" long x 40" circumference

Note: The neckline is gathered and can be adjusted to fit.

INGREDIENTS

½ yard of aqua print for top of dress

½ yard of pink print for dress hem

1 fat quarter of brown polka-dot print for ruffled trim and pocket

Scraps of aqua, pink, and brown prints for flower appliqué and covered button

½ yard of purchased aqua fabric trim or wide rickrack for pocket

2¾ yards of 1⅜"-wide brown satin ribbon for ties

1 button to cover, ⅞" diameter

PREP WORK

From the aqua print, cut:

1 strip, 15" x 42"; crosscut into
2 pieces, 15" x 20½"

From the pink print, cut:

1 strip, 16½" x 40½"

From the brown polka-dot print, cut:

4 strips, 3¼" x 21"

1 rectangle, 4" x 10½"

From *each* of the aqua and pink scraps, cut:

10 flower petals (pattern is on page 41)

From the brown satin ribbon, cut:

2 pieces, 48" long

ASSEMBLY

1. Layer the two aqua strips right sides together. On each end of the strips, measure in 2¼" from the end and 6" down from the top; mark both places with a pencil. Align your rotary-cutting ruler with these two points and cut off the fabric at an angle for the armholes (fig. A).

2. Turn under a narrow hem along each angled cut on the aqua rectangles and stitch in place to finish the armholes (fig. B). Then turn under a narrow hem along the top edge of each aqua rectangle. Stitch. On each rectangle, fold this edge to the wrong side of the aqua fabric, making a 1¼" fold. Press, and then stitch in place along the hemmed edge to make a casing.

3. Sew the aqua rectangles right sides together along the short edges to form the bodice of the dress. Zigzag or serge the seam allowances to finish the raw edges.

4. Sew the pink strip right sides together along the short ends. Finish the seam allowances. Then fold this fabric tube in half *wrong sides together*, with the unfinished raw edges even (fig. C). Press the folded edge flat for the hem of the dress.

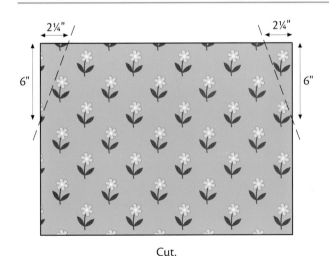

Cut.

Fig. A

Hem diagonal corners.

Fig. B

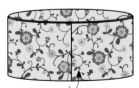

Fold and press.

Fig. C

39

5. Sew the pink fabric to the bottom edge of the aqua dress, right sides together. Finish the seam allowances as before.

6. Sew the brown polka-dot 3¼"-wide strips together end to end. Then refer to step 3 on page 88 to make ruffled brown trim. Sew the trim to the dress along the seam line between the aqua and pink fabric.

7. To make the pocket, fold the brown polka-dot 4" x 10½" rectangle in half, right sides together. Stitch around the edges using a ¼" seam allowance, leaving the bottom open for turning. Turn right side out and press flat. Pin the pocket to the hem portion of the dress front, approximately midway between the brown trim and the hemline. Stitch in place around the sides and bottom. Cover the seam line with purchased fabric trim or with wide rickrack. Stitch through the center of the trim to attach it around the side and bottom edges of the pocket.

8. Sew the pink and aqua petals together in pairs of different or matching colors, sewing them right sides together and leaving the flat edge open for turning. Turn each right side out and press flat. Using a hand-sewing needle and thread, run a basting stitch along each open petal end and pull to gather slightly (fig. D). Sew the five aqua petals to the pocket, making sure not so sew through to the dress layer. Add the five pink petals on top. Make a covered button using the scrap of brown print and stitch to the center of the flower.

9. Attach a safety pin to one end of a length of brown ribbon and use it to thread the ribbon through one of the casings at the top of the dress. Repeat for the other ribbon and casing. Pull the ribbons to gather the neckline of the dress and tie in bows at the shoulders.

Turn and gather petals.

Fig. D

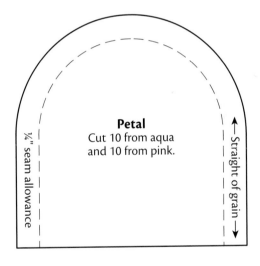

Petal
Cut 10 from aqua
and 10 from pink.

¼" seam allowance

← Straight of grain →

GIFTS
for Teens and Tweens

It's inevitable that every young person goes through an "I've gotta be me" phase. You'll be the favorite gift-giver of all with any teen or tween by creating a gift made specifically for her or him. I've included projects that my own emerging "individuals" have used to decorate their personal spaces.

Paper Roses Quilt

Quilting becomes personalized for the teenaged girl in your life with this remarkable pattern. My daughters and their friends love the idea of random strips of fabric and bold, fun trim, which gives this quilt its untraditional look. It's a work of art that will be the centerpiece of any young woman's bedroom.

43

SERVING SIZE

1 quilt, 81" x 81" (excluding ruffles)

INGREDIENTS

Yardage is based on 42"-wide fabric unless otherwise noted.

1 yard *each* of 8 assorted black-and-white print fabrics

2 yards of bright pink solid for center panel

2 yards of pink satin for ruffle

1½ yards of white-with-black print for outer border

½ yard of black solid for inner border

¼ yard of black satin for leaf appliqués

4½ yards of jumbo black rickrack

1 yard *each* of narrow (⅛" wide) ribbon in black-and-white and pink-and-white

9¼ yards of 1"-wide pink pleated trim

5 yards of backing fabric

87" x 87" piece of batting

¾ yard of fusible web

PREPARATION

From the assorted black-and-white print fabrics, cut:

42 strips, 2⅞" x 42"; cut each strip in half to yield 84 strips, 2⅞" x 21"

8 strips, 1½" x 42"

From the bright pink solid fabric, cut from the *lengthwise* grain:

1 panel, 18" x 69"

1 panel, 14" x 69"

From the white-with-black print, cut:

8 strips, 6" x 42"

From the black solid, cut:
7 strips, 2" x 42"

From the pink satin, cut:
9 strips, 5" x 58"

MAKING THE QUILT

Piecing the Panels

1. Randomly selecting fabrics, sew the 2⅞"-wide strips together end to end in sets of three. Make 28 of these. From each long strip, trim 8" from one end (fig. A); set these extra bits aside as they aren't needed for this project.

2. Randomly sew the strip sets together so that the trimmed ends alternate from one end of the quilt top to the other (fig. B). Press all the seam allowances in the same direction and set aside.

Making the Appliqués

1. Using the patterns on foldout pattern page 1, cut two large, one medium, and two small pentagon shapes from the leftover yardage of assorted black-and-white fabrics.

2. Working log-cabin style, sew a 1½"-wide strip to one side of a pentagon. Trim the strip even with the end of the pentagon (fig. C). Press the seam allowance toward the strip.

3. Turn the pentagon and sew a different 1½" strip to the pentagon. Continue in this manner, sewing, pressing, and trimming, until you have finished two complete rounds around each pentagon (fig. D). Carefully press under ¼" around the perimeter of each pentagon. Set aside.

4. Using the circle patterns on pattern page 1, trace two large and four small circles onto fusible web. Iron the fusible web onto the wrong side of leftover assorted black-and-white print fabrics and cut out the circles on the drawn lines. Set aside.

5. Using the leaf patterns on pattern page 1, cut two large, two large reversed, six small, and six small reversed leaves from the black satin. Pairing two of the same-sized leaves right sides together, stitch around the leaves using a ¼" seam allowance and leaving the flat bottom of each leaf open for turning. Turn the leaves right sides out and press lightly with a *cool* iron or finger-press. Take care not to singe or melt the satin.

21" Trim. 8"

Make 28.

Fig. A

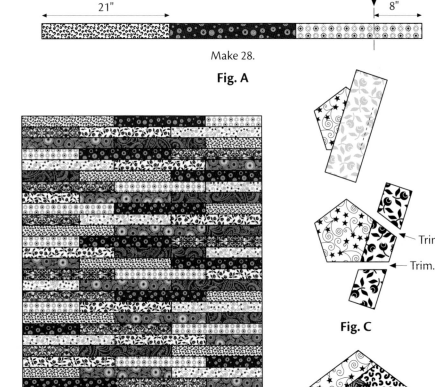

Fig. B

Trim.

Trim.

Fig. C

Make 2 large, 1 medium, and 2 small.

Fig. D

6. Topstitch veins on each leaf as indicated on the leaf patterns (fig. E).

Appliquéing the Panel

1. Referring to the quilt photograph, on page 44, position the pentagons, leaves, and circles on the 18"-wide pink panels. Make sure to leave plenty of room around the long edges of the panel; these will be trimmed into curved edges later. Once you are satisfied with the positioning, use your iron to fuse the circles in place. Pin the other pieces to hold them.

2. Cut the narrow ribbons into 8" lengths. Fold each piece of ribbon in half and position the ribbons as desired on top of or near the black leaves, tucking the ends of the ribbons under the pentagon edges. Pin or baste in place.

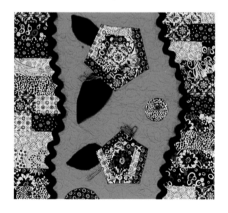

3. Using the blanket-stitch feature on your machine (or whatever decorative stitch you like!) and black thread, stitch around the perimeter of each circle and pentagon. Make sure the raw edges of the satin leaves are hidden under the pentagon flowers so that the stitching will secure the leaves too. Leave the other edges of the leaves and ribbons unsecured.

Joining the Panels

1. Cut the black-and-white quilt top apart lengthwise so that you have one piece that is approximately 18" wide and one piece that is approximately 36" wide. This doesn't have to be exact.

2. Measure the length of the black-and-white panels. They should be approximately 60" long. Trim both pink panels to this length.

3. Sew the black-and-white panels to either side of the plain 14"-wide pink panel. Take care to align the strips across the width of the pink panel so that your quilt top will remain square and true.

4. Referring to the quilt photo and using your rotary cutter and cutting mat, trim the edges of the 18"-wide appliquéd panel to give each long edge undulating curved edges. Make sure that the curves are only a few inches deep: you don't want to make this panel narrower than the 14" pink panel.

5. Position the appliquéd panel over the pink panel on the quilt top. Make sure the pink panel below is completely covered. Pin, and then machine baste the raw edges of the appliqué panel in place.

6. Position the black rickrack over the raw edges of the pink appliqué panel, centering the rickrack on top of the raw edges. Pin, and then stitch in place. This will conceal and secure the raw edges as well as add a decorative element.

Adding the Borders

1. Sew the 2"-wide black solid strips together end to end. Measure the length of the quilt and from the long black strip, cut two borders to this length. Sew the borders to the sides of the quilt top and press the seam allowances toward the borders.

2. Measure the width of the quilt top and trim the remaining border fabric into two pieces of this length. Sew them to the top and bottom of the quilt and press.

3. Sew the 6"-wide white-with-black print strips together end to end in pairs. Measure the length of the quilt top and trim two of the borders to this length. Sew these borders to the sides of the quilt top.

4. Measure the width of the quilt top, trim the remaining two borders to this length, and join them as for the other borders. Press.

Leave open.   Topstitch.

Fig. E

Finishing Details

1. Trim the corners of the quilt top to round them off. A small saucer or dish will help you mark smooth curves.

2. Layer and baste the quilt top, batting, and backing and machine quilt as desired. Or take your project to your favorite long-arm quilter for quilting. *Just be sure to leave ½" of fabric unquilted all the way around the quilt for adding the ruffles and finishing the edges.*

3. To make the satin ruffle, sew the 5"-wide pink satin strips together end to end. Press the seam allowances open using a cool iron. Then fold the long strip in half, right sides together, to conceal the seam allowances. Press.

4. Using the longest stitch length on your machine, machine baste the raw edges of the satin ruffle, stitching first ⅜" from the edge, and then ⅛" from the edge. Pull the thread tails on the underside (the bobbin thread) to gather the ruffle to fit the perimeter of the quilt top (fig. F). You'll need approximately 325" of ruffle.

5. With right sides together, align the raw edges of the purchased pink pleated trim with the edges of the quilt top. Machine baste in place, *sewing through the quilt top and batting only.* Fold the backing fabric out of the way. Then place the pink ruffle atop the pleated trim and baste in place in the same manner, adjusting gathers in ruffles as needed to fit (fig. G).

6. Fold the ruffles and pleats back to check for puckers. Make any adjustments, and then machine stitch in place to secure.

7. Trim the *batting only* close to the stitching (fig. H).

8. Fold the trim back, away from the quilt top, and turn the seam allowance in toward the batting (fig. I). Press lightly on the right side.

9. Turn the seam allowance of the backing fabric under ¼" and pin the fold to the back side of the ruffle, covering the seam allowance and stitching line. Hand stitch in place (fig. J).

10. Hand tack the leaves in place, taking just a few hidden stitches underneath to prevent them from flopping back. Let the ribbon trim hang free.

Pull to gather.

Fig. F

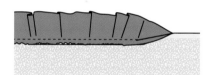

Fig. I

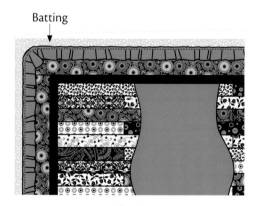

Batting

Fig. G

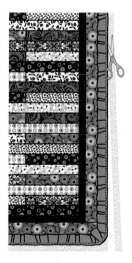

Fig. H

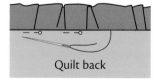

Quilt back

Fig. J

PAPER ROSES QUILT

47

With the "Paper Roses" quilt on page 43 complete, here are ideas for coordinating accessories that will make your teen or tween's room a standout. Pillow shams, a satin rose pillow, a fun purse pillow, and a purchased bed skirt customized with satin ruffles will complete the whole look that no girl could resist.

Paper Roses Shams, Pillows, and Bed Skirt

SERVING SIZES

2 Euro shams, 24" x 24"

1 satin rose pillow, 18" diameter x 4" deep

1 purse pillow, 15½" x 11½", excluding handle

1 bed skirt, queen size (60" x 80")

INGREDIENTS

Yardage is based on 42"-wide cotton fabric and 58"-wide satin (unless otherwise specified).

Shams:

1¾ yards of hot pink cotton for shams

1½ yards of muslin for lining

Scraps of black and white prints for circle appliqués (use leftovers from quilt on page 43)

2 squares of batting, 25" x 25"

2 pillow forms, 24" x 24"

Rose pillow:

1 yard of pink solid cotton for pillow

1¾ yards of pink glitter satin (58" wide) for ruffled rose

14" or 16" pink zipper

1 pillow form, 18" diameter, or polyfil for stuffing

1 faceted gem, 1⅛" diameter

Glue gun and hot-glue sticks

Purse pillow:

⅝ yard of pink solid cotton for pillow front and back and purse-flap lining

⅜ yard of pink glitter satin for purse flap

½ yard of muslin for pillow lining

⅛ yard of black tulle

Scraps of black velveteen and black-and-white cotton print for embellishment

12½" x 16½" piece of batting

12" x 16" rectangular pillow form

20" length of ⅝"-diameter cotton cording

1 faceted gem, ¾" diameter

1 snap or 1" square of Velcro

Bed skirt:

1 purchased queen-size, tailored, black cotton or cotton-polyester blend bed skirt (it will be covered, so color isn't critical, but look for one with flat sides rather than ruffled)

9¼ yards of crepe-backed black satin (44" wide) for ruffles

PREP WORK

Shams (makes 2):

From the hot pink cotton, cut:
4 pieces, 17" x 24½"
2 pieces, 25" x 25"
8 strips, 1¼" x 15"

From the muslin, cut:
2 pieces, 25" x 25"

From the black and white scraps, cut:
12 white strips, 1¼" wide; lengths can vary from 4" to 6"
9 black strips, 1¼" wide; lengths can vary from 4" to 6"
3 black squares, 5½" x 5½"

Rose pillow:

From the pink solid cotton, cut:
2 circles, 19" in diameter
2 strips, 4½" x 29¼"

From the pink glitter satin, cut:
8 yards (288") total of 7"-wide bias strips

Purse pillow (makes 1):

From the pink solid cotton, cut:
2 rectangles, 12½" x 16½"
1 rectangle, 8" x 16½"
2 strips, 2" x 16"

From the pink glitter satin, cut:
1 rectangle, 8" x 16½"
1 bias strip, 2¼" x 16½"

From the muslin, cut:
1 piece, 12½" x 16½"

Bed skirt:

From the crepe-backed black satin, cut:
2 lengths, 120" long; cut each piece in half lengthwise to yield 4 pieces, 22" x 120"
1 length, 90" long; cut in half lengthwise to yield 2 pieces, 22" x 90"

MAKING THE PILLOW SHAMS

1. Layer a 25" pink square with batting and a 25" muslin square. Baste with safety pins or thread, and then machine quilt as desired. The pillow shams shown here were quilted in a large meandering pattern. Make two. Trim the quilted squares to 24½" x 24½".

2. To make the appliquéd black-and-white circles, sew the 1¼"-wide strips together, alternating white and black strips as shown. Use the shortest strips on the outer edges and the longest ones in the center.

Make three strip sets for each sham, each with seven strips (fig. A).

3. Layer each strip set right sides together with a black square. Using the pillow sham circle pattern on pattern page 1, trace a circle onto the wrong side of the top fabric. Stitch all the way around the circle on the drawn line. Trim away the excess fabric, leaving a ¼" seam allowance (fig. B). Make a slit in the black fabric, taking care not to cut into the strip-pieced fabric. Turn the large circle right side out through the slit and press flat. Make three dots for each sham.

4. Position the circles in a row along one end of the quilted pillow-sham top, with the outer two circles 3½" from the top and sides and the remaining circle centered between them (fig. C). Stitch the circles in place by hand or machine.

5. Fold the 1¼"-wide pink strips in half lengthwise, right sides together, and stitch a narrow seam along the long edge and across one short end of each. Turn right side out and press flat to make the pillow ties.

6. Machine stitch a narrow hem along one 24½" side of each of the 17" x 24½" pink rectangles. On two of the rectangles, sew a tie to the inside of the hemmed edge, positioning each 8" in from the sides. On the remaining two rectangles, position the ties along the unhemmed 24½" edge, 8" in from the sides. Machine baste in place (fig. D).

Make 3 per sham.

Fig. A

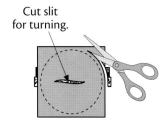

Cut slit for turning.

Trim, leaving ¼" seam allowance.

Fig. B

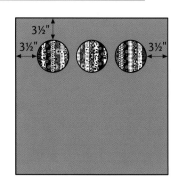

3½"

3½"

3½"

Fig. C

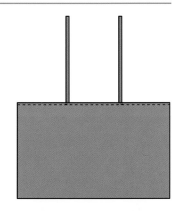

Make 2 each.

Fig. D

7. Lay the quilted pillow sham right side up on your sewing table. Lay a rectangle with ties attached to the hem edge on top, aligning the raw edges. Then lay a rectangle with the ties at the cut edge on top, aligning the raw edges at the opposite end of the pillow. Pin, and then stitch all around the pillow using a ½" seam allowance. Trim the corners and turn the pillow sham right side out (fig. E).

8. Insert the pillow form into the sham and tie closed.

9. Repeat all steps to make two pillow shams.

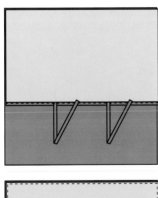

Stitch completely around
sham layers.

Fig. E

MAKING THE SATIN ROSE PILLOW

This tuffet-style pillow is covered with a zippered pink cotton cover. Gathered satin strips are added to make a rose motif on the top for the epitome of girly indulgence!

1. Sew the two 4½" pink cotton strips together along their short edges using a ½" seam to make a strip 4½" x 57". Machine baste one of the pink circles and the 54" pink strip together for about 18" (fig. F). This is just a partial seam so that you can insert the zipper. Press the seam allowance open.

2. Place the closed zipper face down on the seam allowance (on the inside/wrong side of the pillow pieces). Pin or hand baste in place. Then, using a zipper foot, machine stitch each side of the zipper tape to the pillow pieces (fig. G).

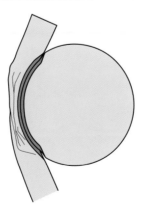

Baste seam for 18".
Press open.

Fig. F

Stitch on each side
of zipper tape.

Fig. G

3. Sew the two short ends of the 57½" pink strip right sides together using a ¼" seam allowance. Press the seam to one side.

4. Pin the now-joined strip to the remainder of the pink circle, easing to fit as necessary. Machine stitch a ¼" seam allowance. Press.

5. Before joining the other pink circle to the pillow cover, attach the pink satin strips to form the rose. Sew the 7"-wide bias strips together end to end to make a strip approximately 8 yards long. Press the seam allowances open. Fold the strip in half lengthwise, wrong sides together, and press using a warm iron.

6. Machine baste two rows of stitching along the long raw edges, ¼" apart, to gather the long strip so that it is lightly ruffled.

7. Machine stitch the ruffle to the pillow, starting by placing the beginning end of the ruffled strip so that the outer folded edge extends slightly beyond the edge of the circle. Stitch along the gathered edge to secure the ruffle to the pink circle. As you approach the end of the circle, begin moving the ruffle in closer toward the center of the circle, positioning the strip

so that the ruffle edge covers the previous stitching and raw edge by about 1" to 1¼" (fig. H). Continue sewing. If you prefer, you can cut the threads, remove the pillow from the machine, and pin the next round of the ruffled strip in place before stitching.

8. Continue circling the pillow top in this manner, sewing the ruffle closer toward the center of the circle until you have reached the center. Backstitch and remove from the machine.

9. To cover the stitching at the center of the pillow, glue a large faceted gem to the pillow.

10. Open the zipper (and remove the basting stitches along that seam) to give better access as you sew the decorated pink circle to the other side of the 54" pink ring. Pin the edge of the pink cotton circle to the remaining raw edge of the ring, taking care to keep the ruffled edges away from the stitching area. Sew the seam, and then turn the pillow right side out through the zipper opening.

11. Insert the pillow form or polyfil, fluff the ruffle, and voilà! A satin rose pillow.

MAKING THE PURSE PILLOW

1. Layer the 12½" x 16½" muslin, batting, and pink solid cotton. Machine quilt as desired. I used an allover meandering pattern to quilt the layers together. Square up the edges when the quilting is complete.

2. Fold the 2" x 16½" pink cotton strip in half lengthwise, wrong sides together, and press. Attach this binding strip to one long edge of the quilted fabric from step 1. The bound edge will be the top edge of the pillow that will be covered by the purse flap.

3. On the wrong side of the 8" x 16½" pink solid rectangle, mark the purse flap by measuring 3¼" down from the top edge on each short end and 7½" down from the midpoint of the long edge as shown. Connect the marks using a pencil and ruler (fig. I). This will be your stitching line.

4. Position the marked pink rectangle right sides together with the satin rectangle. Stitch on the marked V, pivoting at the bottom of the V.

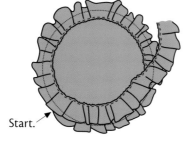

Start.

Stitch ruffle to pink circle, extending edge of ruffle beyond circle.

Fig. H

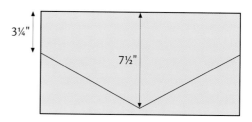

3¼"

7½"

Mark stitching line.

Fig. I

Trim the excess fabric, leaving a ¼" seam allowance. Clip the excess fabric from the point (fig. J), and then turn right side out and press flat. Press from the cotton side or use a cool iron so you don't melt or scorch the satin.

5. To make the handle, fold the pink satin bias strip in half lengthwise, right sides together. Stitch a ¼" seam allowance along the long edge. Sew one end of this inside-out tube to one end of the ⅝"-diameter cotton cording. Then slip the tube over the cording,

turning it right side out with the cording inside (fig. K). Trim to 18½" long.

6. Lay the unquilted 12" x 16½" pink rectangle right side up on your table. Position the ends of the handle from step 5 along the top edge of the rectangle, with raw edges aligned and the handle on top of the pink fabric as shown. The handle ends should be about ⅜" from the side edge. Machine baste in place (fig. L).

7. Layer the satin purse flap right side down on top of it, aligning the top and side raw edges. Pin in place. Finally, layer the quilted purse front on top, right side down, aligning the bottom and side raw edges. The bound edge will be overlapping the purse flap. Stitch all the way around the layered pieces using a ¼" seam allowance. Stitch slowly as you go over the handles; there will be a lot of bulk at these points. Trim the excess fabric and batting from the corners, and then turn right side out.

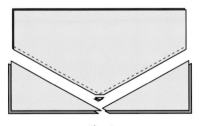

Fig. J

Stitch tube to end of cording.

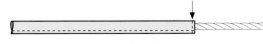

Fig. K

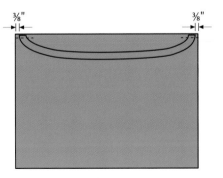

Baste.

Fig. L

8. Sew a snap or small piece of Velcro on the inside of the flap point and along the front of the pillow to correspond. Insert the pillow form into the pillow covering and snap or seal the Velcro to close.

9. To decorate the pillow, make a layered and gathered fabric flower as shown. First, fold the tulle in half lengthwise and run a row of basting stitches along the long raw edges to gather it into a circle that's approximately 6" in diameter. Knot to secure. Using the patterns on pattern page 1, cut a large flower from black velveteen a small flower from a scrap of black-and-white cotton print. Layer each of these on top of the black tulle circle, working from largest at the bottom to the smallest on top. Tack the layers together, stitching to the point of the purse flap to secure. As a finishing touch, make and attach a pink satin yo-yo (see page 35, step 6), and then glue a faceted gem to the center of the flower.

MAKING THE SATIN BED SKIRT

1. Fold each length of black satin in half lengthwise, right sides together. Stitch along one short end and along the long raw edges (fig. M). Turn the fabric right side out. Fold in the seam allowance at the open short end and stitch closed by machine. Repeat for all four pieces of black satin.

2. Draw a chalk line approximately 10½" from the bottom edge of one side of the bed skirt. Position the top (seamed edge) of one of the 120"-long black satin pieces along this line and stitch in place, pleating the fabric every 1½" (fig. N).

3. In the same manner, stitch another 120"-long black satin piece just below the seam line on the black cotton bed skirt where the side is joined to the under-the-mattress panel (fig. O). This top ruffle will cover the stitching line of the bottom ruffle.

EASY PLEATS

If you have a ruffler or pleating attachment for your sewing machine, you can use it to pleat the black satin panels while sewing them to the bed skirt. If you don't have this type of attachment, you can simply pleat the fabric as you go.

4. Repeat steps 2 and 3 to attach ruffles to the other long side of the bed skirt. Then add the two 90" lengths of black satin to the foot end of the bed skirt.

Leave open for turning.

Fig. M

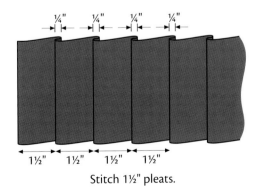

¼"   ¼"   ¼"   ¼"

1½"   1½"   1½"   1½"

Stitch 1½" pleats.

Fig. N

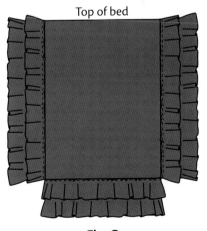

Top of bed

Fig. O

Rock 'n' roll, country, jazz, pop, and every musical style in between can be celebrated with this quilt. Personalize it to your music fan's favorite style with appliqués of the instrument he or she is learning to play, or even a microphone for those lead singers in your life. This is a chart-topping gift for any music-loving guy or a girl.

"Record This!" Quilt

SERVING SIZE

1 quilt, 70½" x 97"

12 Courthouse Steps blocks, 13" x 13"

4 Record blocks, 13" x 13"

INGREDIENTS

Yardage is based on 42"-wide fabric unless otherwise noted.

2⅝ yards of black print for appliqués, music staff, inner border, piano keys, and binding

2¼ yards of gray print for outer border

1⅝ yards of white solid for music staff and piano keys

⅞ yard of blue print for Courthouse Steps blocks

⅞ yard of green print for Courthouse Steps blocks

⅞ yard of light plaid for Courthouse Steps and Record blocks

½ yard of light brown print for Courthouse Steps blocks

½ yard of light rust print for Courthouse Steps blocks

¼ yard of rust solid for Record blocks

5½ yards of backing fabric

76" x 103" piece of batting

2½ yards of fusible web

4 black buttons, ¾" diameter

PREP WORK

From the blue print fabric, cut:

6 strips, 2½" x 42"; crosscut into:

    12 pieces, 2½" x 6½"

    12 pieces, 2½" x 10½"

6 strips, 2" x 42"; crosscut into

12 pieces, 2" x 13½"

From the green print fabric, cut:

6 strips, 2½" x 42"; crosscut into:

    12 pieces, 2½" x 6½"

    12 pieces, 2½" x 10½"

6 strips, 2" x 42"; crosscut into

12 pieces, 2" x 13½"

From the light brown print fabric, cut:

6 strips, 2½" x 42"; crosscut into:

    12 pieces, 2½" x 10½"

    12 pieces, 2½" x 6½"

    12 squares, 2½" x 2½"

From the light rust print, cut:

6 strips, 2½" x 42"; crosscut into:

    12 pieces, 2½" x 10½"

    12 pieces, 2½" x 6½"

    12 squares, 2½" x 2½"

From the light plaid, cut:

1 strip, 2½" x 42"; crosscut into

12 squares, 2½" x 2½"

4 squares, 14" x 14"

From the black print, cut from the *lengthwise* grain:

5 strips, 2" x 52½"

5 strips, 2¼" x 52½"

6 strips, 2½" x 58"

1 strip, 3¾" x 45"

From the white solid, cut from the *lengthwise* grain:

4 pieces, 5¼" x 52½"

1 strip, 4¾" x 45"

18 pieces, 1⅜" x 8"

From the gray print, cut on the *lengthwise* grain:

4 strips, 8" x 75"

4 strips, 8" x 15½"

PIECING THE COURTHOUSE STEPS BLOCKS

Instructions are for making one block. Repeat to make a total of 12 blocks.

1. Sew together 2½" light brown, light plaid, and rust print squares. Press the seam allowances toward the darker fabrics (fig. A).

2. Rotate the unit from step 1 so that the brown square is on top and the rust square is on the bottom. Then sew a 6½" green strip to the right side of the unit from step 1 and a 6½" blue strip to the left side. Always press the seam allowances toward the newly added pieces (fig. B).

3. Sew a 6½" light brown strip to the top of the block and a 6½" light rust strip to the bottom. Press (fig. C).

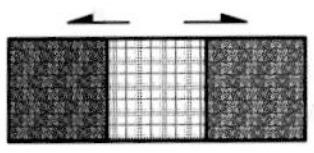

Fig. A

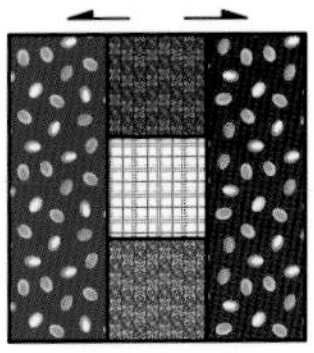

Fig. B

Fig. C

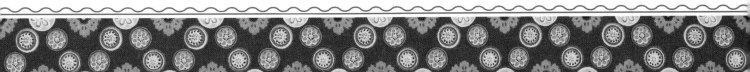

"RECORD THIS!" QUILT

4. Add the 10½" green and blue strips to the block as in step 2 on page 57. Press. Then add the 10½" light brown and light rust strips to the block as in step 3. Press.

5. To complete the block, add the 13½" green and blue strips (fig. D). Press. The completed block should measure 13½" x 13½".

APPLIQUÉING THE RECORD BLOCKS

Instructions are for making one block. Repeat to make a total of four blocks. The patterns for the record pieces are on pattern page 3. Prepare the appliqué shapes for hand or fusible appliqué. You'll need four of circle A for the black record and four of circle B for the rust solid record center.

1. Fold a 14" light plaid square in half in each direction and crease lightly to mark the center.

2. Center the black circle on the square and appliqué in place.

3. Repeat with the rust solid circle.

4. Press the block and trim to 13½" x 13½" (fig. E).

MAKING THE MUSIC STAFF PANEL

Sew the 5¼" x 52" white strips together with the 2" x 52" black strips, alternating them as shown. Press the seam allowances toward the black strips (fig. F). The appliqués will be added after the quilt top has been assembled.

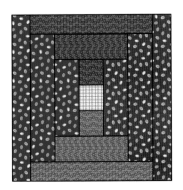

Courthouse Steps block.
Make 12.

Fig. D

Fig. F

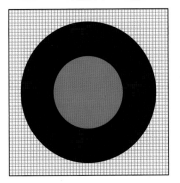

Record block.
Make 4.

Fig. E

PUTTING IT
ALL TOGETHER

1. Lay out the pieced and appliquéd blocks in rows as shown. You'll have two rows with a Record block at each end and two rows with only Courthouse Steps blocks. Make sure to rotate the blocks as shown to match the color placement. Sew the blocks together in rows. Press (fig. G).

2. Sew rows 1 and 2 together, and then join the musical staff panel. To complete the quilt top interior, add rows 3 and 4 to the bottom of the staff. Press.

3. Prepare the musical notes, the G-clef, and the instruments for appliqué following the instructions on pattern page 3. In the quilt shown, these pieces were fused in place, and then stitched using a machine blanket stitch. Refer to the quilt photo on page 58 for placement ideas.

MAKING SOFT MUSIC

To keep the quilt fabrics as soft and pliable as possible, for the larger appliqué pieces don't use fusible webbing on the entire shape. A bit of fusible web around the perimeter of the record, for example, is enough to do the trick. The edges can be fused in place, and then stitched by machine for security. The center of the shape will remain completely flexible.

4. Measure the width of the quilt, which should be 52½". Trim two of the black 2¼"-wide strips to the same length as the quilt width and sew them to the top and bottom of the quilt. Cut one of the remaining 2¼"-wide black strips in half. Sew a half strip to both of the remaining 2¼"-wide strips. Trim these long strips to the length of the quilt, which should be 82½". Sew the strips to the sides of the quilt. Press all seam allowances toward the black borders.

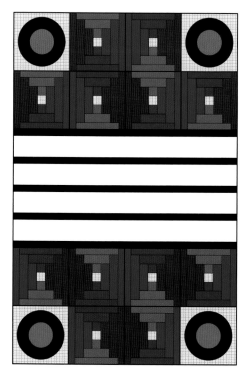

Fig. G

5. To make the piano-key borders, sew a 3¾"-wide black strip to a 4¾"-wide white strip. Make two. Press the seam allowance toward the black strips. From these strip sets, cut eight segments, 3⅛" wide, and eight segments, 2¼" wide (fig. H).

6. Sew the segments from step 5 together with 1⅜" x 8" white pieces in the sequence shown below. Make two of these borders. Sew an 8" x 15½" gray piece to each end of each border strip (fig. I).

7. Sew the piano-key borders to the top and bottom of the quilt, making sure that they're oriented correctly. Press the seam allowances toward the black inner border.

8. Sew the remaining gray 8"-wide strips together in pairs. Measure the length of the quilt top and trim the borders to this length. Sew the borders to the sides of the quilt and press the seam allowances toward the black inner borders.

FINISHING TOUCHES

1. If you plan to do your own quilting by hand or machine, layer the quilt backing, batting, and quilt top together and baste. Otherwise, you can simply deliver the quilt top and backing fabric to your favorite long-arm machine quilter.

2. The quilt shown has the words "Hit Me With Music" quilted in the white portions of the musical staff. The quilt also features straight-line quilting in the piano-key border to divide the wider black/white segments into three piano keys and the narrower ones into two piano keys.

3. Sew a black button to the center of each record.

4. Bind the quilt using the 2½"-wide black strips.

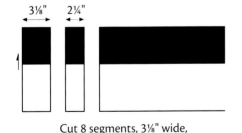

Cut 8 segments, 3⅛" wide, and 8 segments, 2¼" wide.

Fig. H

Make 2.

Fig. I

Give teens a classy way to organize their electronic gadgets with this made-to-order charging station. This is a purchased item that I simply embellished to coordinate with the "Record This!" quilt on page 57, but you can choose a fabric to match any decor. This is a good project for some get-together time with the teens.

Charging Station

SERVING SIZE

1 charging station, 12½" x 9" x 6½"

INGREDIENTS

1 purchased charging station (styles and sizes vary)

⅓ yard of gold print fabric

Thin cardboard

Spray adhesive

Brayer or craft stick for smoothing fabric

PREP WORK

From the thin cardboard, cut:

2 pieces, 6¼" x 8⅝", or size to fit the sides of charging station

1 piece, 2¾" x 12", or size to fit the front of charging station

From the gold fabric, cut:

2 pieces, 8¼" x 10⅝", or 1" larger all around than the cardboard

1 piece, 4¾" x 14", or 1" larger all around than the cardboard

COVERING THE CHARGING STATION

1. Apply a light coating of spray adhesive to the wrong side of the fabric and to the cardboard piece. Work on just one piece at a time so that the adhesive doesn't dry too quickly.

2. Center the adhesive side of the cardboard on the wrong side of the fabric and press together. Turn over to make sure the fabric is smooth. If there are any wrinkles or bubbles, smooth them out with a brayer or a craft stick.

3. Turn the piece back over to the wrong side. Fold the fabric along the sides to the back and press to the cardboard. Make sure the edges are pulled taut, but not so tight that the fabric is stretched. Repeat for the top and bottom edges, folding the corners at 45° angles to miter them (fig. A).

You can cut away excess fabric at the corners for a flat finish.

4. Repeat steps 1–3 for all fabric pieces.

5. Spray adhesive to the back side of each prepared fabric/cardboard piece and position them on the sides and front of the charging station. You may want to do these one at a time and weight them down until the adhesive has dried before continuing to the next piece.

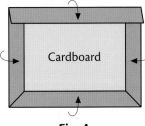

Fig. A

Some kids have a hard time letting go of old T-shirts or sports jerseys. Since it seems impossible for them to part with their favorites, here's a way to display them in a patchwork quilt for their bed. You'll score big points with this gift idea, and you'll enjoy preserving the memories, as well.

T-Shirt Memories Quilt

SERVING SIZE

1 quilt, 84" x 98"

INGREDIENTS

Yardage is based on 42"-wide fabric.

15 favorite T-shirts, with design area measuring 12½" x 12½"

3 yards of blue-and-green print for blocks and outer border

2 yards of blue chambray for sashing and inner border

⅝ yard of tan flannel for blocks

½ yard of blue flannel for block centers

¾ yard of green print for binding

7½ yards of backing fabric

88" x 102" piece of batting

5 yards of 17"-wide lightweight fusible interfacing

PREVENTING PUCKERING

Be sure to prewash your fabrics. The T-shirts will most likely have been washed many times and won't shrink. But flannel tends to shrink quite a bit the first time it's washed. So to avoid a puckering quilt, wash all of the fabrics before cutting and sewing.

PREP WORK

From the blue flannel, cut:
12 squares, 6½" x 6½"

From the tan flannel, cut:
48 squares, 3½" x 3½"

From the blue-and-green print, cut:
8 strips, 3½" x 42"; crosscut into 48 rectangles, 3½" x 6½"
10 strips, 6½" x 42"

From the blue chambray, cut:
7 strips, 2½" x 42"; crosscut into 20 sashing strips, 2½" x 12½"
17 strips, 2½" x 42"

From the green print, cut:
9 binding strips, 2½" x 42"

From the interfacing, cut:
13 squares, 13" x 13"

PREPARING THE T-SHIRTS

1. Carefully cut the front of each T-shirt away from the back and sleeves along the sides. Most T-shirts don't have side seams, so lay the shirts flat and cut with a pair of scissors along the folds at the sides.

2. Lay each square on your ironing board, right side down, and smooth it out. Iron out any wrinkles, and then fuse a square of lightweight interfacing to the wrong side of the T-shirt, centering it over any design.

3. Use your rotary cutter and ruler to cut a 12½" square from each of the prepared T-shirts.

MAKING THE PATCHWORK BLOCKS

1. Sew a 3½" x 6½" blue-and-green rectangle to opposite sides of each blue flannel square. Press the seam allowances toward the rectangles. Make 12.

2. Sew a 3½" tan flannel square to both ends of each remaining blue-and-green rectangle. Press the seam allowances toward the rectangles. Make 24.

3. Sew the units from step 2 to the top and bottom of the units from step 1 to make 15 blocks (fig. A).

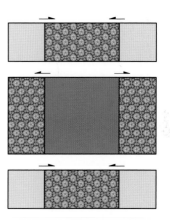
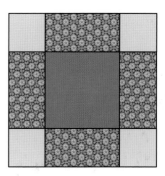

Make 15.

Fig. A

ASSEMBLING THE QUILT TOP

1. Lay out the prepared T-shirt squares and the patchwork blocks in five rows of five blocks each. Alternate the patchwork and T-shirt blocks, rearranging the T-shirts until you're satisfied with the layout.

2. Place a 2½" x 12½" strip of blue chambray vertically between the blocks in each row. Sew the blocks and strips together in rows. Press all seam allowances toward the chambray strips (fig. B).

3. Sew the 42"-long strips of blue chambray together in pairs to make eight long strips. Trim six of these strips to 68½" long, the same length as your block rows. Sew a strip to the top of each block row. Then sew the rows together. Add the remaining chambray strip to the bottom of the quilt top. Press

all seam allowances toward the chambray strips (fig. C).

4. You should have two long chambray strips left. Cut the remaining 42"-long chambray strip in half and sew one piece to each of the remaining long strips. Trim these to the length of your quilt top, which should be 86½". Sew them to the sides of the quilt top.

5. Sew the 6½"-wide blue-and-green print strips together in four pairs. Cut the two remaining 6½" strips in half and sew a half strip to each long pair of strips. Trim two of these strips to 86½" and sew them to the sides of the quilt top. Press. Cut the remaining single blue-and-green strip in half and add a half strip to each of the remaining long blue-and-green strips. Measure the width of the quilt top (it should be 84½") and trim the long border strips to

this length. Sew them to the top and bottom of the quilt top. Press.

FINISHING THE QUILT

1. Cut the backing fabric into three equal-length pieces. Remove the selvages and sew the pieces together side by side. Press the seam allowances to one side.

2. Layer the backing fabric, batting, and quilt top. Baste the layers together and quilt as desired. Or, take the backing and quilt top to your favorite long-arm machine quilter. To go with the sports theme of the T-shirts used in this quilt, my quilter stitched baseballs and basketballs in the blue flannel squares.

3. Trim and square up the quilt, removing all excess batting and backing fabric. Use the 2½"-wide green print strips to make and attach double-fold quilt binding.

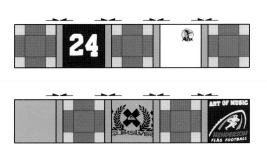

Fig. B

Fig. C

GIFTS
for Your Best Girlfriends—and Mom

What would we do without the women in our lives who encourage our goals, make us laugh, and keep us on track? The gifts I love to give are feminine and pretty but also very practical because I know they'll be used again and again. I love the look on a friend's face when I tell her that the gift was made by me just for her.

Travel Coordinates:
Hanging Accessory Bag and Jewelry Satchel

I first envisioned this gift idea after visiting the dressing room of my friend Mary Hart, the host of *Entertainment Tonight*. She had a plain beige hanging bag filled with stage jewelry. I thought, "Great idea, but what if we take it from bland to bold?" Here's the finished project. It's perfect for travel or for everyday use. It sure saves time when you have to coordinate quickly!

SERVING SIZES

1 hanging accessory bag, 17½" x 44"

1 jewelry satchel, 4½" tall x 4¾" diameter at bottom, when closed

INGREDIENTS

Hanging accessory bag:

1⅜ yards of floral-and-animal print cotton (enough for both projects)

1⅛ yards of black velveteen

⅝ yard of animal-print cotton

1⅛ yards of 18"-wide vinyl

Scraps of black satin for hanger cover

Purchased wooden hanger (flat, not shaped)

Optional jewel-setting tool and assorted crystals for embellishing

Jewelry satchel:

¾ yard of pink satin fabric for interior pockets, edge trim, and drawstring

½ yard of black velveteen or use leftovers from accessory bag

½ yard of black satin fabric for lining

5" square of plastic canvas

PREP WORK

Hanging accessory bag:

From the floral-and-animal print, cut on the *lengthwise* grain:
1 piece, 18" x 44"

From the remaining floral-and-animal print, cut on the *crosswise* grain:
1 piece, 6½" x 18"

4 binding strips, 2¼" x 42"

From the black velveteen, cut:
1 piece, 18" x 38"

From the vinyl, cut:
6 strips, 4¾" x 18"

3 strips, 3" x 18"

From the animal print, cut:
1 piece, 6½" x 18"

20 pieces, 1½" x 18"

Jewelry satchel:

From the black velveteen, cut:
1 circle, 16" diameter

From the black satin, cut:
1 circle, 16" diameter

From the pink satin, cut:
2 circles, 9¾" diameter

110" total of 1"-wide bias strips

From the plastic canvas, cut:
1 circle, 4¾" diameter

MAKING THE HANGING ACCESSORY BAG

1. Fold each 1½" x 18" length of animal print fabric in half lengthwise and press. Fold the long raw edges in toward the center fold and press again.

2. Place a folded strip over *each* long edge of a vinyl pocket strip. Edgestitch in place, sewing through all layers to secure. Repeat for all pocket pieces. Do not turn under the raw edges on the ends; they will be covered by the final binding.

3. Layer the 6½" x 18" animal print and floral-and-animal print strips right sides together. Lay the wooden hanger near the top of these strips so that the base of the hook is 1" from the top edge. Using a fabric marker, trace the shape of the top edge of your hanger onto the fabric (fig. A). Cut away the excess fabric on both strips, leaving a ½" seam allowance above the marked line.

Repeat for the top edge of the 18" x 44" floral-and-animal print rectangle.

4. Sew the bottom edge of this animal print piece to the top edge of the black velveteen fabric (fig. B). Using a warm (not hot) iron, carefully press the seam allowance toward the animal print fabric.

5. Lay the fabric-edged vinyl pockets across the velveteen and pin in place, pinning through the fabric edging and not through the vinyl. The bag shown has the pockets in the following order from top to bottom: two 4¾" pockets, three 3" pockets, and four 4¾" pockets. Use this plan or arrange as desired.

6. Stitch each pocket in place by sewing along the *bottom* fabric edge only, stitching over previous stitching. Then divide the wide pockets into smaller ones by stitching *vertically* through all

pockets. On the project shown, the vertical lines are stitched approximately 4½" apart. Notice that the stitching line on the right starts at the first 3"-deep pocket and doesn't extend into the top two rows of pockets. This provides a few pockets with wider storage space (fig. C).

7. Trim the bottom flat edge of the small floral-and-animal piece from step 3 with animal print binding as you did for the vinyl pockets. Make a small buttonhole or eyelet at the top center of this piece, making sure the buttonhole is not in the seam allowance.

8. Layer the short floral-and-animal print piece right side down followed by the long matching piece, right side down, and finally the vinyl piece right side up. Pin along the edges, and then machine baste the layers together, stitching all the way around using a ¼"-wide seam allowance.

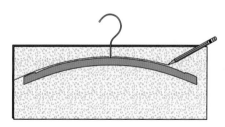

Mark shape of hanger.

Fig. A

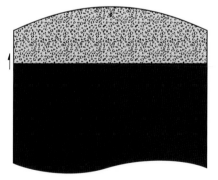

Fig. B

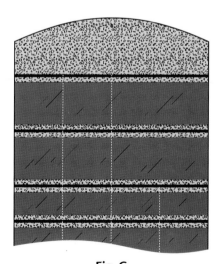

Fig. C

9. Sew the 2¼"-wide floral-and-animal print strips together end to end to make a long binding strip. Fold the strip in half lengthwise, wrong sides together, and press. Fold in the long raw edges as you did for the shorter animal print strips and press. Fold this fabric strip over one long edge of the accessory bag and edgestitch through all layers using a normal stitch length. Trim excess fabric. Repeat for the other long side.

10. Using the leftover animal print strip, add binding to the top and bottom of the bag in the same manner, tucking in the fabric ends as you do so.

11. Embellish or personalize the bag as desired. On my bag, I used leftover strips of pink satin from the jewelry pouch, animal print, and black velveteen to make gathered flowers. Hand stitch the base of each flower to secure. You can stitch or glue them to the top front of the bag. Use a jewel-setting tool to add hot crystals to the fabric flowers.

12. Insert the wooden hanger under the short flap on the back of the bag and poke the hanger through the buttonhole. To cover the metal crook of the hanger, cut a 2"-wide strip of black satin about 12" long. Fold the strip, right sides together, and stitch across one short end and the long edges to make a closed-end tube. Turn the tube right side out and slip onto the hanger, bunching the extra length for a ruched effect. Hand stitch or glue the open end to the top of the accessory bag.

MAKING THE JEWELRY SATCHEL

1. Cut a small slit in the center of one of the pink circles, cutting on the bias so that the opening won't continue to tear when you use it for turning the pieces right side out.

2. Stitch the two pink circles right sides together using a ¼" seam allowance. Sew all the way around the circle, and then turn right side out and press flat. Whipstitch the opening closed. It won't be seen, but this will keep the slit from stretching open as you work.

3. On the black velveteen circle, mark eyelet openings for the drawstring as follows: mark two eyelets about ¼" apart from one another, 1¼" in from the edge of the circle. Then mark two more eyelets in the same fashion on the opposite side of the circle (fig. D). Stitch the eyelets and open the holes.

4. Sew the 1"-wide pink satin bias strips together end to end. From this long strip, cut two lengths, each about 54" long. Fold one of the lengths in half, wrong sides together, and press with a warm iron. Machine baste this pink satin piping around the perimeter of the circle with the eyelets, with the *raw edges even* (fig. E). You may find a zipper foot is helpful for this step.

5. Cut a small slit on the bias of the black satin circle as you did on the pink circle. Then layer the two black circles right sides together and stitch all the way around, stitching ¼" from the edge. Turn right side out through the slit opening. Whipstitch the opening closed. Press flat with a warm iron and with the velveteen face down

on a towel so that you don't crush the fabric nap.

6. To make a casing for the drawstring, stitch 1" from the outer edge of the black circles. Then stitch again, ½" from the first round of stitching.

7. Center the plastic canvas over the black satin circle with the slit in it. Then center the prepared pink circle over that, with the slit side down. Stitch all the way around the plastic canvas circle to secure

the layers.

8. To make individual storage pockets, mark stitching lines from the stitched circle to the outer edge of the pink circle. First divide the circle in half, and then into quarters, and then into eighths. Stitch on each marked line, backstitching on each at the outer edge of the pink circle (fig. F).

9. Fold the remaining length of pink satin bias strip in half, right sides together. Stitch a narrow seam

along the long raw edges. Use a safety pin or bodkin to turn the strip right side out. Using a safety pin through one end of the bias cord, thread it through one of the eyelets around to the opposite side of the circle. Bring the cord out of the first eyelet, and then right back in the adjacent eyelet. Continue weaving it to the final eyelet and bring it out again. Remove the pin and knot the ends of the cord. Draw up the cord from both sets of eyelets to close the bag (fig. G).

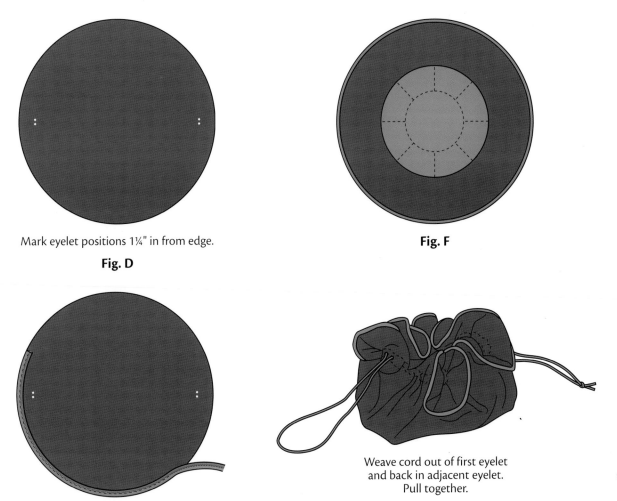

Mark eyelet positions 1¼" in from edge.

Fig. D

Fig. F

Fig. E

Weave cord out of first eyelet and back in adjacent eyelet. Pull together.

Fig. G

 This is, without a doubt, my favorite sewing tote. It's a great gift for any woman who knits, crochets, embroiders, or sews. Personalize it to your own taste with anything from antique buttons to lace. This bag seems to say, "Look at me. I'm fabulous!"

Vintage-Inspired Sewing Tote

SERVING SIZE

1 large tote, 14" wide x 5½" deep x 13" tall, excluding handles

INGREDIENTS

6 to 8 assorted fat quarters for patchwork bottom of bag

1 yard of muslin for interlining

⅝ yard of cream print for bag exterior and handles

⅝ yard of light blue paisley fabric for bag lining

½ yard of tan rose print for handles and pocket linings

½ yard of tan striped fabric for bag and pocket bindings

¼ yard of red polka-dot fabric for interior pockets

¼ yard of tan cotton duck for interior pocket lining

20" x 32" piece of fusible interfacing

2 pieces of batting, 22" x 42" and 8" x 24"

1 piece of plastic canvas, 5½" x 13¾", for bag bottom

Embellishments:

1⅛ yards of ⅞"-wide ecru lace trim

1 lace doily, approximately 11" diameter

2 ecru crocheted lace squares, 2¼" x 2¼"

1 ecru crocheted lace flower, 2" diameter

Scrap of pink felt, flannel, or wool for needle case

1 snap

15 assorted buttons

2 small spools of thread

Assorted colors of embroidery floss

PREP WORK

From the light blue paisley fabric, cut:

1 rectangle, 19½" x 32"

From the red polka-dot fabric, cut:

2 strips, 8" x 19½"

From the tan cotton duck, cut:

2 strips, 8" x 19½"

From the tan rose print, cut:

1 rectangle, 8½" x 6¼"

2 strips, 2½" x 42"

From the tan striped fabric, cut:

1 strip, 1" x 42" (for bow)

2½"-wide bias strips, enough to yield 40"

1 strip, 2¼" x 4½"

MAKING THE TOTE

Use ¼"-wide seam allowances throughout, unless specified otherwise.

Lining and Inside Pockets

1. Sew a red polka-dot and tan duck rectangle right sides together along their long edges. Turn right side out and press flat. Topstitch along one long edge; this will be the top edge of the pocket. Make two.

2. Fuse a piece of interfacing to the blue paisley 19½" x 32" rectangle.

3. Position a red polka-dot pocket 3" from each 19½" edge of the prepared blue rectangle. Stitch in place along the long bottom edge of each pocket. Then divide the pockets by sewing vertically through the center of one pocket and sewing the other vertically into thirds (fig. A).

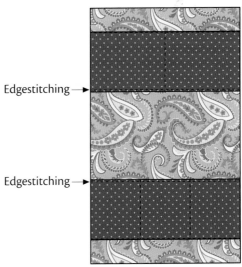

Edgestitching →

Edgestitching →

Stitch interior pockets.

Fig. A

4. Fold the prepared rectangle in half, right sides together, aligning the two 19½" raw edges. Stitch the side seams and press open (fig. B).

5. To miter the lining to make a flat bottom, fold the tote so that the center of the bottom aligns with the seam allowance on one side of the tote lining. (The lining will now be in a triangle shape.) Measure 5½" from the point of the triangle and mark. Sew across the triangle at this 5½" mark, backstitching at each end of the seam (fig. C). Repeat for the other corner of the tote lining. Set the lining aside for now.

Making the Crazy Patchwork
The exterior of the bag has a Crazy-pieced bottom. Create two pieces, 24" x 8", for the bottom of the bag and the heart pincushion.

1. From the assorted fat quarters, cut strips at random angles. Sew the strips together in random color order, sewing groups of three strips together at a time. The shape will be irregular. Crosscut the Crazy strip pieces, again using angles other than the typical 90° (fig. D).

2. Mix up these pieces and sew them back together in sets of three to make 16 Crazy Nine Patch blocks. Trim the blocks to 6½" square (fig. E). Sew the blocks together in two rows of four blocks each. Sew the rows together to make a piece of Crazy patchwork that is at least 8" x 24" (fig. F). Repeat to make a second patchwork piece.

3. Press the Crazy patchwork, then layer each one with a piece of batting and muslin backing fabric. Machine quilt the entire piece. My bag was quilted in an allover meandering pattern.

4. From the quilted Crazy patchwork, cut two pieces, 19½" x 7½". From the remainder, cut one heart shape using the pattern on pattern page 4. Set the heart aside. Sew the 19½" x 7½" pieces into a tube by stitching them together along their short ends. Press the seam allowances open.

Assembling the Bag Exterior
1. Like the bag bottom, the top portions and exterior pockets are also quilted. Layer the cream print with batting and muslin backing

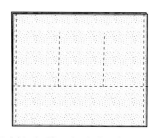

Fold in half and stitch side seams.

Fig. B

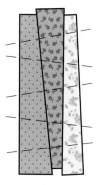

Fig. D

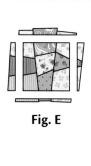

Fig. E

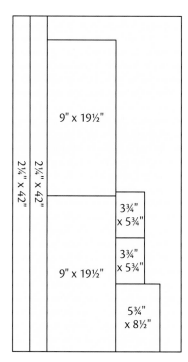

9" x 19½"

2¼" x 42"

2¼" x 42"

3¾" x 5¾"

3¾" x 5¾"

9" x 19½"

5¾" x 8½"

Cutting for quilted fabric

Fig. G

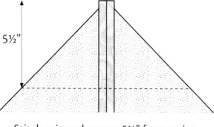

5½"

Stitch mitered corner 5½" from point.

Fig. C

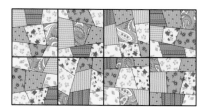

Make 2.

Fig. F

fabric. Meander quilt by machine. Then from this quilted fabric, use figure G to cut the following:

2 handles, 2¼" x 42"

2 pieces, 9" x 19½"

2 pockets, 3¾" x 5¾"

1 pocket, 5¾" x 8½"

2. If you want to embroider the pockets, it's easiest to do that now, before the bag is assembled. The designs for the large and small pocket embroidery are on pattern page 4. Don't add the buttons until after the bag is complete.

3. Using the tan striped 2¼" x 4½" strip, bind the top edge of one of the 3¾" x 5¾" pockets. Tuck in the ends of the binding to hide the raw edges. In the same manner, bind the other small pocket using the tan rose print 2¼" x 4½" strips.

4. To bind and line the large pocket in one step, lay the tan rose print 8½" x 6¼" piece right sides together with the embroidered 8½" x 5¾" pocket. Stitch along the top edge of the pocket. Flip the tan print fabric up and over the pocket. Smooth out and machine baste the layers together along the outer edges (fig. H).

5. Position the large pocket on one of the quilted cream rectangles, centering the pocket from side to side and aligning the bottom edges. Stitch in place, sewing ⅛" from the side and bottom edges (fig. I). The stitching will later be covered.

6. To line the quilted bag handles, sew a tan rose print 2½" x 42" strip right sides together with a handle, stitching along the long edges only. Turn right side out, press, and edgestitch on both long edges. Repeat for the other handle.

7. Position the handles 5" in from the outer edges of the bag front so that they cover the raw edges of the large pocket. Making sure they are not twisted, pin the handles to the bag, aligning the bottom raw edges. Machine stitch along both edges from the bottom of the handles to the top of the pocket. Repeat for the other side of bag, sewing the remaining handle to the remaining quilted cream rectangle.

8. Sew the bag front to the back, right sides together. Stitch along the short ends. Press the seam allowances open.

9. Pin the two smaller pockets to the bag top, centering each of them over a side seam and with the bottom raw edges aligned. Zigzag stitch the pockets to the bag, using a narrow stitch width to secure the pockets and prevent the raw edges from fraying (fig. J).

Stitch.

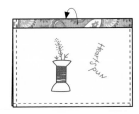

Machine baste along side and bottom edges.

Fig. H

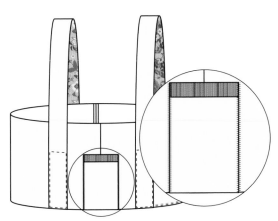

Zigzag stitch pockets over side seams.

Fig. J

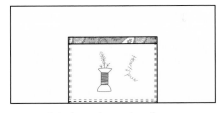

Stitch pocket to bag front.

Fig. I

10. Sew the Crazy patchwork tube to the bottom of the cream bag exterior. Press the seam allowances to one side, and then stitch the length of 7/8"-wide ecru lace trim over the seam on the outside of the bag (fig. K).

11. Sew the bottom of the bag closed, and then miter the bag bottom as you did for the bag lining (see step 5 on page 76).

FINISHING THE BAG

1. Insert the piece of plastic canvas into the bottom of the bag so that it lies flat on the bottom.

2. Insert the bag lining into the bag, wrong sides together. Adjust the lining so that the side seam allowances are aligned with those of the bag. Pin along the top edge, and then machine baste the layers together.

3. Cut the doily in half, handling it carefully so that the edges don't unravel. Center one half at the top of the bag front and the other half at the top center of the bag back. Pin in place, and then machine stitch to secure.

4. Using the pattern on pattern page 4, cut two tab pieces from one of the fat-quarter scraps. Sew the tab pieces right sides together, leaving the short straight end open for turning. Turn right side out and press. Make a machine buttonhole lengthwise in the tab to accommodate the size of button you've selected for the closure. Cut the buttonhole open (fig. L). Position the tab along the center top edge of the bag back, raw edges aligned. Baste in place.

5. Using the tan striped bias strips, bind the top edge of the bag to secure all the layers, including the doilies. Flip the buttonhole tab up and toward the front of the bag. You may want to hand stitch it to the binding so that it stays in the forward position.

6. Sew a button to the front of the bag to correspond with the buttonhole tab to close the bag.

FINISHING DETAILS

The bag shown here is decorated with embroidery details, which were added before assembling the bag (see step 2 on page 77). Now's the time to add all the buttons to the flower stems. In addition, my bag features a needle case and a pincushion.

1. To make the heart pincushion, retrieve the Crazy patchwork heart you set aside earlier. Cut another heart out of scrap fabric for the back. With wrong sides together, blanket-stitch the two hearts together using embroidery floss, leaving an opening for stuffing (fig. M).

2. Fill the heart with batting scraps, and then complete the blanket stitching.

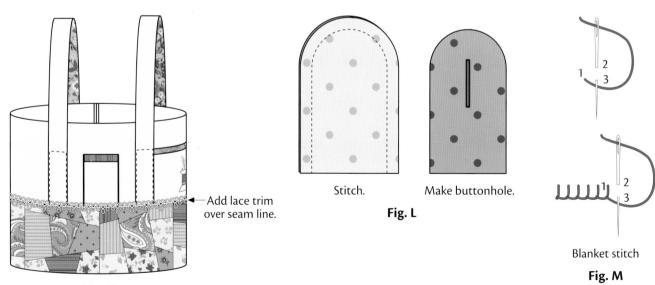

Add lace trim over seam line.

Fig. K

Stitch. Make buttonhole.

Fig. L

Blanket stitch

Fig. M

3. Attach the small crocheted flower to the center of the heart by stitching a button on top of it and through all layers to secure. Hand sew or glue the pincushion to the front of the bag, referring to the photo on page 74 for placement ideas.

4. To make the needle case, cut a piece of pink felt, 3¼" x 6½", and a rectangle from one of the fat-quarter fabrics, 3¼" x 6½". Sew them right sides together, leaving an opening for turning. Turn right side out and press. Edgestitch around the entire needle case.

5. Center a tan striped 1" x 42" strip over the center of the needle case on the felt side. Turn under the raw edges and stitch along both sides to secure the strip to the needle case. Leave the remaining raw edges unsewn (fig. N).

6. Fold the needle case in half to close, with the felt on the inside.

Add a snap closure.

7. On the outside, stitch the small crocheted square to the front of the needle case and add a decorative button. Bring the ends of the tan striped strip together on the outside of the needle case and tie in a

bow. Thread each end of the tie through a spool of thread and knot the end of the tie to secure.

8. Sew or glue the needle case to the outside of the bag.

9. Add any remaining buttons, embroidery, or decorative elements you desire!

Stitch strip to needle case.

Fig. N

This elegant book cover, made from a pale fabric with a printed metallic design, is perfect for protecting your Scriptures or even the novel you're reading. I made one for my journal and have also covered photo albums for friends. The ruched flower and faceted gem embellishments enhance to the rich look of this easy-to-make gift. The instructions here are for a cover to fit a 6" x 9" book, but you can adjust the measurements accordingly for a larger or smaller volume.

Elegant Book Cover

SERVING SIZE

1 book cover, 16" x 10" when open

INGREDIENTS

⅝ yard of gray or silver cotton fabric

⅛ yard of pink print fabric

10½" x 21½" piece of fusible interfacing

1 yard of ⅞"-wide gray wire-edged satin ribbon for bookmark

Embellishments:

1 jeweled butterfly, approximately 1¾" x 1"

1 faceted clear gem, ⅜" diameter

1 faceted gem, ⅛" diameter

PREP WORK

From the gray or silver fabric, cut:
2 rectangles, 10½" x 21½"

From the pink fabric, cut:
2 strips, 1" x 42"

ASSEMBLING THE BOOK COVER

Use a ¼" seam allowance throughout.

1. Iron fusible interfacing onto the wrong side of one of the gray rectangles.

2. Place the gray rectangles right sides together and stitch along both short ends and along the top and bottom edges, keeping the first and last 5" unsewn (fig. A). Turn right side out through one of the openings and press flat.

3. If desired, add quilting stitches to hold the layers together. There is no batting, but you can still quilt!

4. Fold each short edge toward the outside of the book cover by 2½". The raw edges of the openings should match up. Machine stitch the folds in place, stitching along the top and bottom seam lines. Stitch again to secure, and then trim the seam close to the stitching (fig. B). Turn the corners right side out and press.

5. Mark the position where you'd like your ruched flower to be. Simply mark the outer circle for a starting point with a pencil or fabric marking pen. It won't show in the end.

6. Sew the pink strips together end to end. Fold in half lengthwise and press. Sewing by hand, baste along the raw edges to gather. Pull up the gather, and then position one end of the strip around the marked circle, making sure the folded edge extends beyond the circle to cover it. Hand stitch the strip to the book cover. Continue coiling the gathered strip, working your way in to the center of the circle and tacking in place by hand (fig. C).

7. Glue the large gem in the center of the ruched circle. Hand sew the jeweled butterfly where desired and add the small gem to finish the look. Fold the ribbon in half and hand sew or glue the folded edge to the inside top center of the book cover to act as a bookmark.

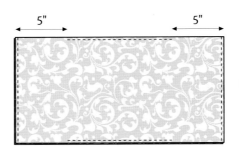

5"   5"

Stitch, leaving 5" open at each end of top and bottom.

Fig. A

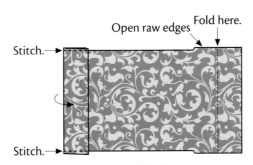

Open raw edges   Fold here.

Stitch. →

Stitch. →

Fig. B

Hand stitch ruching in place, using marked circle as a guide.

Fig. C

I made a personal family tree pillow for my mother, years ago, featuring each of my brothers' names, and even appliquéd their favorite hobbies to their branches. My mother was thrilled with it. In this example, family members' names and important aspects of their lives are embroidered by machine, and symbols are added with appliqué—a quilt block, home, church, a heart, and more. It's a unique gift idea for a newlywed bride. She can add leaves as her family grows.

Family Tree Pillow

SERVING SIZE

1 pillow, 16" x 16"

INGREDIENTS

½ yard of red paisley print for border and pillow backing

Fat quarter of cream print for background

Fat quarter of brown print for tree appliqué

¼ yard of green print for grass and leaves

⅛ yard of red print for border and appliqués

Scraps of assorted greens for leaves

Scraps of red, cream, tan, brown, and black wool or felt for appliqués

Black embroidery floss for hand embroidery or black thread for machine embroidery

16" pillow form

PREP WORK

Using the patterns on pattern page 3, prepare the appliqué pieces for your favorite method of appliqué. The pillow shown was hand appliquéd.

From the cream print, cut:
1 square, 12½" x 12½"

From the green print and green scraps, cut:
1 grass section
25 leaves*

* If you plan to embroider by machine, you may need to embroider the names on the green fabric first, and then cut out the leaves.

From the brown print, cut:
1 tree

From the red print, cut:
2 strips, 1¼" x 12½"
2 strips, 1¼" x 14"
4 squares, 1¼" x 1¼"
1 heart

From the paisley print, cut:
1 square, 16½" x 16½"
2 strips, 1½" x 14"
2 strips, 1½" x 16½"
5 squares, 1¼" x 1¼"

From the wool or felt scraps, cut:
Home, hand, church, and musical note appliqués

ASSEMBLING THE PILLOW

1. Position the grass over the cream square and align the bottom and side edges. Appliqué the top curve in place and baste the remaining edges together.

2. Embroider the family names on the leaves by hand or machine; you may want to do this before cutting out the leaves.

3. Prepare the other design elements from the wool or felt pieces. Stitch the 1¼" red and paisley squares together into a small Nine Patch quilt block; sew the heart to the hand; and sew the windows, doors, and roofs to the house and church.

4. Position the tree and appliqué in place. Then position the leaves and other elements on the branches as desired. When you like the arrangement, appliqué each of the pieces in place.

5. Add the remaining embroidery details, stitching meaningful words for your family as desired. In my pillow, I've used Family, Home, Faith, Service, Love, Family, God, Music, and Prayer.

6. When all the appliqué and embroidery is complete, press the pillow top. Then add the red border strips as follows: sew the shorter strips to the top and bottom of the pillow; press the seam allowances toward the borders. Then add the side borders and press. Repeat for the paisley strips.

7. Position the pillow top right sides together with the large paisley square. (The square may be larger than the pillow top; just center the pillow top.) Sew the two pieces together, stitching ¼" from the edges of the pillow top and leaving a 10" opening along the bottom edge for inserting the pillow form. Trim any excess fabric from the paisley seam allowance and clip the corners. Turn the pillow cover right side out and press.

8. Insert the pillow form, and then turn under the seam allowances along the opening and hand stitch to close.

Why buy an apron when you can have so much fun making one? Aprons were the anticipated gift that my mother would make for all of her daughters-in-law. The perfect accessory for baking cookies, doing laundry, or any other housework is a fun tiered ruffled apron tied around your waist. Or, for the cook who gets in up to her elbows, make the scalloped apron with attached dishtowel for hand wiping. The green floral apron and hand towels make a lovely gift ensemble, and the matching mother and child aprons become a perfect pair for kiddie cooking lessons.

Aprons, Aprons, Aprons!

SERVING SIZE

1 black-and-white ruffled apron, 19" at waist (plus ties) x 16" long

1 aqua apron with attached towel, 18" at waist (plus ties) x 22" long

1 green floral apron, 18" at waist (plus ties) x 32" long

2 green floral hand towels, 19½" x 23½", including prairie points

1 mommy apron, 13" at waist (plus ties) x 25" total length

1 child apron, 13" at waist (plus ties) x 21" total length

BLACK-AND-WHITE RUFFLED APRON

Ingredients

½ yard of white print for apron foundation and 1 ruffle

½ yard of black print for waistband, ties, and 1 ruffle

¼ yard of white print for 1 ruffle

¼ yard of black print for 1 ruffle

Prep Work

From the ½ yard of white print, cut:
1 rectangle, 10½" x 23½"
1 strip, 5" x 36"

From the ½ yard of black print, cut:
1 strip, 5" x 36"
1 strip, 4" x 19½"
2 strips, 2" x 27"

From the remaining white print and black print, cut:
1 strip, 5" x 36" (2 total)

Making the Apron

1. Lay the 10½" x 23½" white print rectangle on your cutting mat. Measure in 2" from each corner on the top edge. With your rotary cutter and ruler, angle the sides of the apron base by cutting from the bottom corner to the 2" mark along the top (fig. A). This is the apron base.

2. On all four of the 5" x 36" strips for ruffles, machine stitch a narrow hem along both short ends and along one long edge. Then using a long machine stitch, sew two rows of basting threads along the unhemmed edge of each strip, sewing ¼" and ⅝" from the edge of the strip (fig. B). Pull up the bobbin threads to gather. Or see "Dental Floss to the Rescue" on page 88 for a gathering shortcut.

3. Sew one of the black ruffles to the bottom of the apron base, right sides together, adjusting gathers to fit (fig. C). Serge, overcast, or zigzag stitch over the seam to prevent the raw edges from fraying.

4. Measure 3" up from the black ruffle and mark a chalk line (fig. D). Position one of the white ruffles along this line, right sides together with the gathered edge against the line. Stitch in place, adjusting the gathers to fit.

5. Repeat step 4 to sew the remaining black ruffle 3" above the white ruffle.

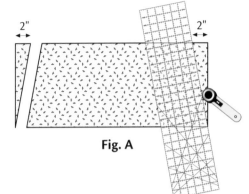

Fig. A

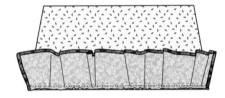

Fig. B

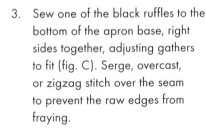

Fig. C

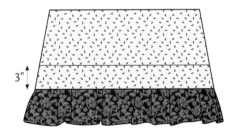

Mark line 3" above ruffle.

Fig. D

6. Machine baste the remaining white ruffle to the top edge of the apron foundation. This seam will be covered by the waistband.

7. To make the waistband, fold the 4" x 19½" black strip in half, wrong sides together; press. Press under ¼" along one long edge of the waistband to the *wrong side* (fig. E).

8. Make the ties by folding the 2" x 27" black strips in half lengthwise, right sides together. Sew along one short end and the long edge with a ¼" seam allowance. Turn right side out and press.

9. Pin a tie to each end of the waistband from step 7 so that the raw edges along the short ends are even. Stitch along both short ends of the waistband using a ¼" seam allowance to secure the ties, but take care to keep the tie ends out of the way. Turn the waistband right side out and press.

10. Pin the flat edge of the waistband (not the edge with the pressed-under seam allowance) to the top of the apron, right sides together. Stitch in place. Flip the waistband up and over the seam allowance. Pin the pressed-under seam allowance over the seam on the inside of the apron, making sure it covers the seam entirely. From the right side of the apron, stitch in the ditch of the waistband to secure it on the inside (fig. F).

Fig. E

¼"

Edgestitch through
all layers of waistband.

Fig. F

MAKE IT A FIESTA!

You choose how to mix and match the colored ruffles any way you'd like in this easy yet tons-of-fun apron. To make a variation like the one shown here, instead of cutting ruffle strips 5" wide like in the black-and-white apron, you'll need to choose three fabrics for your ruffles and cut three strips, 2¼" x 36", from each one. Sew the strips together in strip sets (one strip of each fabric), press all the seam allowances toward the bottom, and then make a narrow hem on the bottom strip and gather the top strip. The combination possibilities are endless.

Prep Work

From the aqua print, cut on the *lengthwise* grain:

1 piece, 20½" x 36"

From the brown floral print, cut:

2 pieces, 6" x 29"

1 piece, 4" x 15" (width of towel plus ½")

1 square, 4" x 4"

From the brown polka-dot fabric, cut:

7 strips, 2½" x 42"

From the tea towel:

Cut in half so that you have a piece approximately 15" to 16" long

Making the Apron

1. Using the scallop pattern on pattern page 4, mark and cut five scallops along the 36"-wide bottom edge of the aqua 20½" x 36" piece (fig. A).

2. Using the packaged seam binding, slip the prefolded binding over the side and bottom raw edges of the apron and edgestitch in place. Miter the corners at the inside corners of the scallops as you go. *Note:* The binding won't show in the finished project; it's just to encase the raw edges.

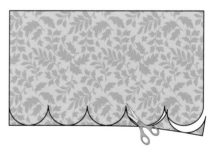

Mark and cut scalloped edge.

Fig. A

AQUA APRON WITH ATTACHED TOWEL

Ingredients

1⅛ yards of aqua print for apron

⅝ yard of brown polka-dot print for ruched trim

⅜ yard of brown floral print for waistband, ties, and towel bands

3¼ yards of ⅜"-wide rose velvet rickrack

4" scrap of pink fabric for covered button

1 purchased white tea towel, approximately 15" x 30"

1 button to cover, 1½" diameter

3" of ¾"-wide sew-on Velcro

1 package of white double-fold seam binding

Optional: gathering or ruching foot for sewing machine

3. Fold each brown polka-dot 2½"-wide strip in half lengthwise, right sides together. Sew a ¼" seam along the long raw edges. Turn right side out and press flat, centering the seam along the back side. Using a gathering foot on your sewing machine if you have one, stitch along the lengthwise center of each brown tube to gather (fig. B).

Note: If you have a gathering foot that will gather one fabric while stitching onto another, you can gather and apply this trim directly to the sides and bottom scalloped edges of the aqua apron in one step. If you don't have any sort of gathering foot, see the tip box at right for a quick and easy way to gather fabric.

Stitch through center and pull threads to gather.

Fig. B

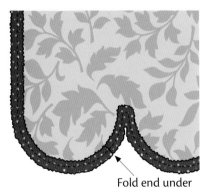

Fold end under to join new strip.

Fig. D

DENTAL FLOSS TO THE RESCUE

If you don't have a gathering foot, you can gather the lengths of brown trim by using dental floss and a zigzag stitch on your sewing machine. Set the machine to a narrow zigzag so that the rickrack will cover it later—but not too narrow that you can't stitch completely over a length of dental floss without sewing into the floss.

Lay the floss along the lengthwise center of the brown tube. Place the beginning of the tube under the machine presser foot and zigzag stitch so that the stitches go back and forth over the floss, but don't catch the floss. Stitch to the end of the brown tube, cut the threads, and cut the floss. Now pull the ends of the floss to pull up the gathers (fig. C). How easy is that?!

Repeat for each brown strip.

Zigzag stitch over floss. Pull floss to gather.

Fig. C

4. Place a brown ruched strip, seam side down, along the bound edge of the apron. Machine stitch in place through the center of the strip. When you reach the end of one strip, lay another strip in place, folding under about ¼" at the end and overlapping it with the raw edges of the previous strip (fig. D). Continue sewing and adding strips in this manner until all edges except the apron top have been covered.

5. Center the rose velvet rickrack on top of the brown ruched fabric and stitch in place using matching thread.

6. Sew the two brown floral 6" x 29" strips together end to end to make a long waistband/tie piece. Press the seam allowances open. Fold the long strip in half lengthwise, right sides together. Stitch across one short end of the strip and for about 20" along the long edge. Repeat for the other end of the strip, leaving the center 18" open (fig. E). Turn right side out and press flat, turning under the two seam allowances at the center opening.

7. Gather the top edge of the apron (see "Dental Floss to the Rescue," left) to 18" wide to fit the opening of the waistband/ties. Insert the raw edge of the apron in the opening of the waistband/ties and adjust to fit. Pin in place, and then machine stitch across the bottom edge of the waistband to secure

Leave 18" open.

Fig. E

(fig. F). Continue topstitching all the way around the waistband/ties. This will prevent the seams from rolling.

8. Measure the width of your towel and trim the brown floral 4" x 15" strip to that measurement plus ½". Fold the strip in half, right sides together, and stitch across the short ends using a ¼" seam allowance. Turn right side out and press flat. Press under ¼" along the open edges. Insert one end of the towel into the trimed piece. Pin in place and edgestitch to secure. Cover the seam line with another strip of ruched brown polka-dot fabric and pink velvet rickrack.

9. Fold the brown floral 4" square in half, right sides together. Stitch the two side seams using a ½" seam allowance. Press under ¼" along the raw edges and turn the piece right side out; press flat. Gather the top edge of the towel and insert into the open end. Edgestitch in place.

10. Position a 3" strip of Velcro on the waistband of the apron, 3" from the left edge of the apron (as you're looking at it) and about 1½" down from the top of the waistband. Stitch in place (fig. G). Sew the other half of the Velcro strip to the wrong side of the brown fabric at the top of the towel. Cover a 1½"-diameter button with pink fabric and make a 2½"-diameter yo-yo from the aqua fabric (see page 98, step 5). Sew these in place to cover the stitching area on the brown fabric at the top of the towel. Secure the towel to the apron with the Velcro.

TOWELS FOR LEFTIES

If this apron is for a left-handed friend, position the towel on the right side of the apron (as you're looking at it) rather than on the left.

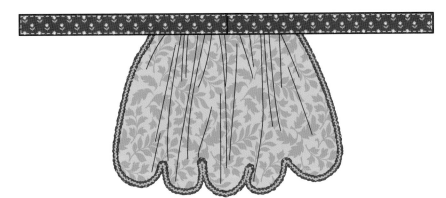

Fig. F

Fig. G

MOMMY AND ME APRONS

These matching aprons look complex but are actually easy to make. You're sure to receive a lot of compliments—especially from the mommy who will love this duo. It's a perfect gift for kids who paint, do crafts, build science projects, cook, or even volunteer to wash the dishes.

make in a weekend

Ingredients

Yardage is sufficient for making both aprons.

1⅛ yards of green floral print for middle ruffles and neckline ties

⅞ yard of cream-and-blue diagonal striped fabric for bottom and neckline ruffles

⅔ yard of pink print for apron bibs and bib linings

½ yard of cream-and-blue polka-dot fabric for apron skirts

½ yard of blue floral print for top ruffles

10¼ yards of ⅝"-wide pink satin ribbon for ties and trim

Prep Work

From the pink print, cut:
2 squares, 16" x 16", for large bib and lining

2 rectangles, 6" x 12", for small bib and lining

From the cream-and-blue polka-dot fabric, cut:
1 strip, 13" x 42"; from this strip, cut:

   1 rectangle, 13" x 24", for large apron skirt

   1 rectangle, 9½" x 20", for small apron skirt

From the blue floral print, cut:
1 strip, 7½" x 39", for large apron top ruffle

1 strip, 5" x 27", for small apron top ruffle

From the green floral print, cut:
1 strip, 10½" x 42", for large apron middle ruffle

1 strip, 6½" x 37", for small apron middle ruffle

From the remaining green floral print, cut on the bias:
92" total of 1½"-wide strips (50" for large apron and 42" for small apron)

From the cream-and-blue diagonal striped fabric, cut:
1 strip, 13" x 42", for large apron bottom ruffle

1 strip, 9" x 42", for small apron bottom ruffle

90

1 strip, 3½" x 42"; from this strip, cut:

 1 strip, 3½" x 18½", for large apron neckline ruffle

 1 strip, 2¼" x 16", for small apron neckline ruffle

Making the Mommy Apron

1. Place the two pink 16" squares right sides together. Using the apron bib pattern on pattern page 4, trace the bib outline on the wrong side of the top square. Stitch on the marked lines on the apron sides and bottom, leaving the top open. Trim excess fabric from the sides and the unsewn top, leaving a ¼" seam allowance beyond the marked and stitched lines (fig. A). Turn right side out and press.

2. Turn under ¼", and then turn under ¼" again on each short edge of the following pieces and stitch in place to make a narrow side hem. Press.

   • 13" x 24" cream-and-blue polka-dot fabric

   • 7½" x 39" blue floral print

   • 10½" x 42" green floral print

   • 13" x 42" cream-and-blue diagonal striped fabric

3. Before gathering the ruffled tiers, zigzag or overcast stitch the bottom long edge of all pieces, except for the polka-dot piece. Then use a straight stitch to sew a length of pink ribbon to cover the overcast edge of each piece (fig. B). Gather the top edge of each tier, including the polka-dot tier.

4. Adjust the gathers on the polka-dot and blue floral tiers so that the pieces are the same width as the bottom of the pink bib. Lay the polka-dot tier on the table, right side up, and then place the blue floral ruffle on top, also right side up, aligning the gathered edges. Place the bottom edge of the pink bib on top of the ruffles so that the bottom edge of the bib overlaps the gathering stitches. Pin the layers together, and then stitch. Add a second row of stitching inside the first to secure the waist of the apron (fig. C).

5. Fold the top blue floral tier out of the way and position the green floral tier halfway between the top and bottom edges of the polka-dot apron skirt. (The top raw edges will be hidden by the blue tier once it's back in place.) Adjust the gathers to fit, and then stitch the green ruffled tier in place (fig D).

6. Sew the diagonal striped tier to the bottom of the polka-dot apron skirt, again adjusting gathers to fit.

Finish raw edge at bottom.

Add ribbon trim.

Fig. B

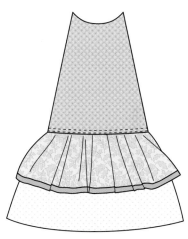

Overlap bib with top gathered edge of ruffles. Stitch.

Fig. C

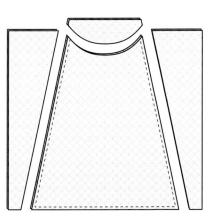

Stitch sides and bottom. Trim excess.

Fig. A

Stitch.

8½"

Fig. D

7. Make a narrow hem on both short ends and one long end of the cream-and-blue diagonal striped 3½" x 18½" strip. Gather the remaining long edge.

8. Position the gathered strip along the raw edges at the neckline of the pink apron bib, adjusting gathers to fit. Baste in place.

9. Sew the green floral bias strips together end to end. Fold in half lengthwise and press. Fold the raw edges in toward the center fold line and press again (fig. E). Refold along the center line. From this length, cut a prepared strip, 50" long.

10. Matching the center of the apron neckline and the center of the bias strip, encase the raw edges of the neckline in the binding. Pin in place, and then edgestitch along all raw edges of the binding (fig. F).

11. Cut two 39" lengths of pink ribbon for the waistline ties. Fold under ½" on one end of each tie and stitch in place to the bottom sides of the pink bib (fig. G). Cut the other end of each tie on the diagonal to prevent fraying.

Making the Little Girl Apron

This apron is made just like the large apron using the smaller pieces listed in the "Prep Work" section on page 90. Below are the only exceptions:

- Use the bib pattern on pattern page 4 to prepare the smaller bib.

- For the neckline tie, you'll need 42" of green floral bias strip.

- Cut the waistline ties 28" long and attach them to the polka-dot apron skirt, 1½" below the bottom of the pink bib.

GREEN FLORAL APRON AND COORDINATING TEA TOWELS

Ingredients

1⅜ yards of green floral print for apron and tea towels

1¼ yards of pink striped print for apron ties, apron hem, and towel trimmings

1 yard of brown polka-dot fabric for apron trimmings and tea towels

1 button to cover, ½" diameter

1" square of Velcro fastener for closure

Prep Work

From the green floral print, cut:

2 strips, 6" x 42"; crosscut into 4 strips, 6" x 20"

1 rectangle, 15" x 33"

1 rectangle, 13½" x 19"

1 rectangle, 9½" x 13½"

1 strip, 4½" x 24"

From the pink striped print, cut:

1 strip, 7" x 33"

2 strips, 6½" x 26½"

1 rectangle, 4" x 12½"

2 strips, 8" x 20"

2 strips, 2½" x 42"

2 apron waistbands using the pattern on pattern page 4; cut on fold as noted

From the brown polka-dot fabric, cut:

1 strip, 16½" x 42"; crosscut into 2 rectangles, 16½" x 20"

2 strips, 2½" x 42"

72" total of 1¼"-wide bias strips

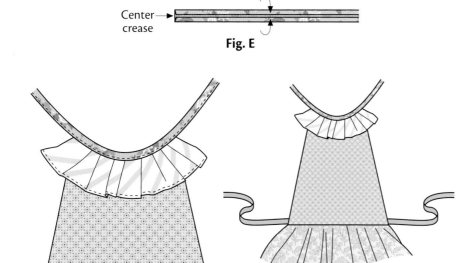

Center → crease

Fig. E

Fig. F

Stitch ties to sides at bottom of bib.

Fig. G

through the center of the ruched brown tube. Cut off the excess ruching and turn under the raw edge at the end of the seam line.

4. Sew the brown 1¼"-wide bias strips together end to end and press the seam allowances open to make one long bias strip. Press under ¼" along one long edge. Then sew the non-folded long edge of the bias to the wrong side of the apron skirt along both side edges and the bottom of the apron using a ¼"-wide seam allowance. Fold the binding to the front of the apron, easing it around the scalloped edges. Press, and then edgestitch to secure, sewing on the right side of the apron.

5. Sew two rows of machine basting stitches along the top edge of the apron skirt. Pull up the bobbin threads to gather the skirt so that it's approximately 19" wide. Set aside.

6. Lay the green 9½" x 13½" rectangle on your cutting mat. Using your rotary cutter and ruler, angle the side edges so that the piece now measures 13½" at the bottom edge and 12½" at the top.

7. Gather both 19" edges of the green 13½" x 19" rectangle (see step 5, above). Adjust the gathers so that the top and bottom edges are the same widths as the top and bottom edges of the bib lining from step 6.

8. Lay the gathered green bib right sides together with the green bib lining. Pin together along the *side edges* (the ones that aren't gathered), taking care to move gathered layers of fabric out of the way. Stitch both side seams using a ¼" seam allowance (fig. A). Turn

Making the Apron

1. Using the pattern on pattern page 4, mark the scallops on the bottom edge of the green floral 15" x 33" rectangle. Cut out, leaving a ½" seam allowance. Mark the scallops on the pink striped 7"-wide strip. Cut out on the line for the bottom edge but leave a ½" seam allowance along the top edge.

2. Turn under the ½" seam allowance along the top edge of the pink striped scallop, clipping the curves

as needed to make a smooth curved edge. Press. Pin the striped scallop on top of the apron skirt so that it overlaps the scalloped edge; then edgestitch to secure.

3. Using the brown polka-dot 2½"-wide strips, make ruched trim referring to "Aqua Apron with Attached Towel" on page 87. Position the ruched trim along the scalloped line to cover the sewing of the pink scallop to the green one. Stitch in place, sewing

right side out and press the seam allowances flat.

9. Position the pink striped 4" x 12½" strip, right sides together, along the top edge of the bib. The seam allowances should extend beyond the side edges of the bib. Stitch along the top edge (fig. B). Press the pink strip up and away from the bib. Remove machine basting if it shows.

10. Fold under ½" along the remaining long edge of the pink strip and press. Then fold the strip in half, right sides together, and stitch the short side seams, taking care not to sew into the bib (fig. C). Turn right side out by flipping the pink strip up and away from the bib. Pin the open edge along the back in place and hand stitch to the bib lining to secure.

11. Sew the remaining ruched brown tube along the seam line between the green print and pink strip at the top of the bib.

12. Press under ¼" along the top curved edge on both waistband pieces. Pin both pieces to the apron skirt, right side facing the front of the apron for one and right side facing the inside of the apron for the other. Adjust apron skirt gathers to fit. Stitch in place using a ½" seam allowance. Stitch both short ends at the side of the waistband, taking care not to catch the apron skirt in the seams (fig. D). Turn right side out and press flat, away from the apron skirt.

13. Insert the apron bib in the top opening of the waistband, centering the bib. (You should have 2½" to 3" of waistband to each side of the bib edges.) Pin in place; then edgestitch to secure.

14. Fold the pink striped 6½" x 26½" apron ties in half lengthwise, right sides together. Stitch along the long edge, and then stitch one end closed, sewing at a 45° angle to make a pointed tie. Trim the excess fabric from the corner and turn the ties right side out (fig. E). Press.

15. Fold a pleat in the unsewn end of each tie so that the depth of the tie matches that of the waistband. Position the ties, right sides together, at the sides of the waistband. Stitch in place using a ¼" seam allowance, and then stitch once more in the seam allowance to secure (fig. F).

16. To make the neck strap, sew the green print 4½" x 24" strip right sides together into a tube. Turn right side out, center the seam allowance along the center of one side, and press flat. Turn in ¼" along each open end and edgestitch to secure.

17. Using scraps of pink fabric, cover a button following the instructions that came with the covered-button kit.

18. Position one end of the neck strap so that the bottom of the strap is flush with the pink striped facing on the inside of the apron bib. Stitch in place to secure. On the other strap end, sew a square of Velcro fastener and sew the

94

Stitch side seams.

Fig. A

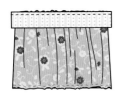

Fig. B

Stitch along short ends.

Fig. C

Fig. D

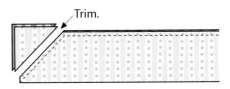

Trim.

Sew end at 45° angle.

Fig. E

Fig. F

corresponding square to the apron bib. Sew the button to the strap only; use the Velcro to open and close the neck strap.

Making the Tea Towels

1. Fold the pink striped 8"-wide strips in half lengthwise, wrong sides together, and press to crease. Open the fold, and then measure and mark 4" squares along one side of the strip. You'll have 2" extra at each end of the strip on one side of the center mark. On the other side of the fold line, measure and mark 4" squares starting at the opposite end of the strip so that the squares are offset. Cut along the marked lines as shown (fig. G).

2. Fold the squares in half diagonally, taking all folds from right to left. Then fold the resulting triangles in half as shown. Finally, flip the triangles on top of the center fold line down to overlap the triangles on the bottom of the fold. Tuck the triangles one inside the other and machine baste along the long straight edge to secure (fig. H). Make two rows of prairie points, one for each towel.

3. Press under ¼" along one 20" edge of each green floral 6" x 20" strip. Lay one of these strips on your sewing table, right side up. Position a row of prairie points along the long edge of the green strip that isn't pressed under, raw edges even. Then lay another green floral rectangle on top, right side down. Stitch along the long edge using a ¼" seam allowance. Stitch the side seams of the green strips, taking care not to catch the prairie points in the seams (fig. I). Repeat for the second towel edging. Turn the green fabric right side out and press away from the prairie points.

4. Stitch a narrow hem on three edges of the brown polka-dot 16½" x 20" rectangles, leaving one 20" edge unstitched. Insert that edge into the opening of the green band from step 3. Pin, and then stitch along the brown fabric to secure. Repeat for the second towel.

5. Fold the pink striped 2½"-wide strip in half lengthwise, right sides together. Sew a ¼" seam along the long edge. Turn the tube right side out and press, centering the seam along the bottom. Make two. Gather the flattened tubes using a gathering foot or by referring to "Dental Floss to the Rescue" on page 88. Adjust the gathers to fit the width of the towel. Position the ruched tube on the towel, centering it over the seam line between the green and brown fabrics. Machine stitch through the center of the strip to secure. Repeat to complete both towels.

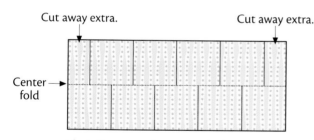

Mark 4" squares. Cut on marked lines to fold.

Fig. G

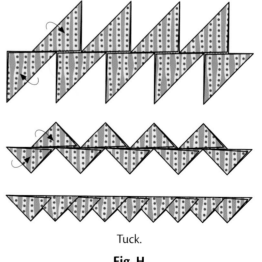

Tuck.

Fig. H

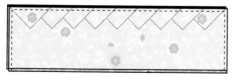

Stitch top and sides.

Fig. I

GIFTS
for Housewarmings and Wedding Showers

What better way to celebrate the seasons of a woman's life than with a handmade gift? From a college apartment, to a new home, to retirement living, the ideas on the pages that follow will make any living space warm and welcoming. Make a project for your own home, and then get ready—you'll soon be receiving gift requests from every woman in your life!

All Buttoned Up
TABLE TOPPER and PLACE MATS

This is an amazing gift for any female family member or friend, from newlywed to grandmother.
I think this scalloped mat with yo-yo trim is the ideal centerpiece for a beautiful table setting.
Then, you can add the coordinating place mats when the girls come over to lunch to chat about
life's yo-yo moments—the ups and downs! Tie a pretty ribbon around the matching napkins for
a pulled-together look. Your dining table will be stunning.

SERVING SIZE

1 table topper, 29¼" diameter

2 place mats, 16¼" diameter

2 napkins, 16" x 16"

INGREDIENTS

8 fat quarters *total* of assorted aqua and teal prints for yo-yos, covered buttons, and binding

2 yards of cream print fabric for table topper, place mats, and napkins

12 buttons to cover, ⅞" diameter, for table topper

16 buttons to cover, ¾" diameter, for place mats

1½ yards of backing fabric

2 pieces of batting, 30" x 30" and 18" x 36"

PREP WORK

From the cream fabric, cut:

1 circle, 30" diameter

2 circles, 17" diameter

2 squares, 17" x 17"

From the assorted aqua and teal fat quarters, refer to figure A to cut:

230" total of 2¼"-wide bias strips

12 squares, 5½" x 5½"

16 squares, 4¾" x 4¾"

MAKING THE TABLE TOPPER

1. Layer the large cream circle with a piece of batting and backing fabric. Pin to baste the layers together. Quilt the layers as desired—I used a large meandering pattern.

2. Using the large scallop pattern, opposite, mark 12 scallops around the perimeter of the quilted cream circle. Cut away all layers along the marked line (fig. B).

3. Sew the aqua and teal 2¼"-wide strips together end to end in a random sequence. Press the seam allowances open. Then fold the long strip in half lengthwise, wrong sides together, to make double-fold binding. Sew the binding to the *wrong* side of the quilted table topper, easing the binding around the scallops and mitering it at the inner corners as you go. Fold the attached binding to the right side of the table topper and machine stitch in place, sewing close to the edge of the binding (fig. C).

4. Using the teal and aqua 5½" squares and the 5" circle pattern on pattern page 1, trim each square into a circle, leaving a ¼" seam allowance outside of the marked circle.

5. Fold the seam allowance of a circle toward the wrong side of the fabric and hand baste in place. Pull up the basting thread to gather. Flatten out the gathered circle, centering the gathering to form a yo-yo. Secure the thread and clip. Repeat for all 12 large yo-yos.

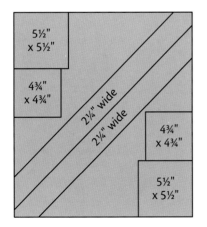

Cutting guide

Fig. A

Trim excess fabric to scallop the edge.

Fig. B

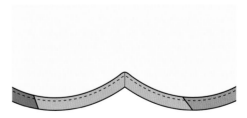

Miter binding at inner corners. Topstitch.

Fig. C

6. Position a yo-yo in each scallop so it's approximately ½" from the bound edge. Hand stitch in place.

7. Following the instructions that come with the covered button kit, use the aqua and teal scraps to cover the ⅞"-diameter buttons. Sew one button in the center of each yo-yo.

MAKING THE PLACE MATS

The place mats are made in exactly the same way as the larger table topper, except they're on a smaller scale. Layer, baste, and quilt the smaller cream circles, and then use the small scallop pattern below to mark and trim the scallops. Bind the place mats as

for the table topper, and then use the 4¾" aqua and cream squares and the medium 4½" circle pattern on pattern page 1 to make 16 yo-yos. Add the yo-yos and ¾"-diameter covered buttons to each scallop.

DRESSING UP THE NAPKINS

To make the napkins, simply fold under and stitch a narrow hem on each edge of the 17" cream squares. If you use a decorative machine stitch to attach the yo-yos to the table topper and place mats, you can repeat the stitch along the hem of the napkins to coordinate.

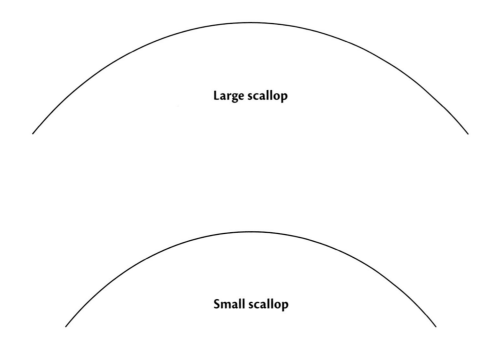

Large scallop

Small scallop

If you can sew a straight line, you can make this fabulous tiered and ruffled shower curtain. All of the layers are simply stitched to a purchased shower curtain, so the base and grommets are already in place! The coordinating towels are also purchased and a favorite trim and fabric hem are added for a super-quick pair of spa-like towels. This is "sew" fun to make that you'll want to create some additional sets to have on hand for last-minute gifts.

Bathroom Spa Ensemble

make in a weekend

SERVING SIZE

1 shower curtain, 70" x 72"

2 bath towels, 30" x 54"

2 hand towels, 16" x 27"

INGREDIENTS

Shower curtain:

1 white standard-sized purchased fabric shower curtain with large grommets for hanging

3⅛ yards of brown rose print

1⅛ yards of pink pin-dot print

1⅛ yards of pink striped fabric

2⅛ yards of pink floral print

1⅛ yards of pink polka-dot print

1⅛ yards of brown-and-pink geometric print

1⅛ yards of brown polka-dot print

Pinking shears or rotary cutter with pinking blade

Towels:

2 bath-sized towels (approximately 30" x 54")

2 hand towels (approximately 16" x 27")

⅝ yard of pink floral print or color to coordinate with towels

2¾ yards of purchased brown pompom trim

Optional: Fray Check fabric sealant

SHOWER CURTAIN PREP WORK

Use a rotary cutter with a pinking blade to cut all strips. All edges are left raw. If you don't have this type of cutter or pinking shears, you'll need to add a narrow hem to all pieces to prevent fraying.

From the brown rose print, cut:
12 strips, 8½" x 42"

From the pink pin-dot print, cut:
4 strips, 8½" x 42"

From the pink striped fabric, cut:
4 strips, 8½" x 42"

From the pink floral print, cut:
8 strips, 8½" x 42"

From the pink polka-dot print, cut:
4 strips, 8½" x 42"

From the brown-and-pink geometric print, cut:
4 strips, 8½" x 42"

From the brown polka-dot print, cut:
4 strips, 8½" x 42"

ASSEMBLING THE SHOWER CURTAIN

All the pinked edges are left raw.

1. Using ¼" seam allowances, sew two matching strips together end to end with *wrong sides together*. Then fold the strips back so they are right sides together and sew the seam again to encase the raw edges of the original seam (fig. A). You've just made a French seam!

2. Using a French seam throughout, sew two more matching strips to the group from step 1 to complete one row. Stitch a long machine basting stitch along one edge of the strip so that you can gather the fabric to the width of the shower curtain.

3. Repeat steps 1 and 2 to make a total of 10 fabric ruffles, each with four strips of fabric.

4. Mark placement lines on the shower curtain using a fabric-marking pen or pencil. Starting at the bottom, mark the first stitching line 6" from the bottom. Then mark additional placement lines approximately 7" apart (fig. B).

5. Decide on the fabric order for your shower curtain. Place the bottom ruffle along the bottom line and pin in place, adjusting the gathers to fit. Machine stitch in place ½" from the pinked edge of the ruffle.

6. Continue adding ruffles in this manner, working from the bottom to the top of the shower curtain.

7. Optional: If desired, you can add purchased trim to coordinate with the towels along the top edge of the shower curtain, just below the grommets, to cover the top row of stitching.

Stitch wrong sides together.

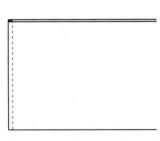

Then stitch again with right sides together to encase raw edges of seam allowance.

Fig. A

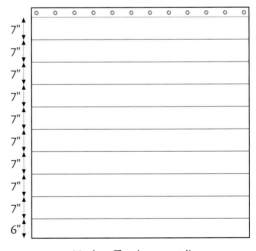

Mark ruffle placement lines.

Fig. B

make it
tonight

3. Gather the strips to fit the width of the towels. Position the strips along one edge of each towel so that the bottom of the strips are approximately 2" from the bottom of the bath towels and 1½" from the bottom of the hand towels. Machine baste in place, stitching between the gathered stitching lines.

4. Cut a length of the pompom trim the width of each towel, leaving a little extra for turning under at the sides. Position the trim to cover the machine basting on the pink ruffles. Machine stitch along the top and bottom of the trim using matching thread. Repeat for all towels.

TOWELS PREP WORK

From the pink floral print, cut:

2 strips, 5" x 42" (1 strip for each bath towel)

2 strips, 5" x 27" (1 strip for each hand towel)

From the brown pompom trim, cut:

2 strips, 31" long (1 strip for each bath towel)

2 strips, 17" long (1 strip for each bath towel)

ASSEMBLING THE TOWELS

1. Make a narrow hem along all edges of each pink floral strip by folding under ¼", and then folding under ¼" again. Stitch in place and press.

2. To gather the strips, stitch one row of machine basting ¾" from the top edge of a pink strip. Sew another row of basting ¼" below the first line. Repeat for all strips.

GIFTS
for Pet Lovers

Even small dogs seem to have great big hearts, which is why we love our pets so much. A heartfelt gift for any adored pup is an appreciated present for its owner, too. These were designed for my mini Maltese, Lola, but I think cat lovers could also make use of this sweet feeding mat.

Pampered Pooch:
Doggy Coat, Leash, and Feeding Mat

Somehow little dogs know how turn up the charm when they're groomed and accessorized, don't they? Here's a fashionable little coat and leash for showing off their style. And every pet owner will love the personalized feeding mat that's vinyl coated for easy cleanup.

SERVING SIZE

1 small dog coat, 4" circumference

1 matching leash, 46" long

1 feeding mat, 18" x 14¾"

INGREDIENTS

Dog coat:

1 fat quarter *each* of 2 coordinating black-and-white prints for dog coat and lining

½ yard of 1¼"-wide purchased pink trim

¾" x 4" piece of fusible interfacing

2 pieces of Velcro fastener: 1½" x 2" and 1⅛" x 2"

1 D-ring, 1" wide

1 purchased pink flower for embellishment (optional)

Feeding mat:

½ yard of white print for feeding mat

½ yard of black print for appliqués and binding

⅛ yard of pink print for appliqués

½ yard of heavy-duty fusible interfacing (Pellon or Timtex)

½ yard of clear vinyl

Leash:

1½ yards of 1"-wide pink nylon webbing

1 swivel bolt snap (available in sewing or craft store with purse supplies)

PREP WORK

Use the dog coat pattern and the appliqué patterns on pattern page 2.

From the black-and-white print for outer coat, cut:

1 coat

From the black-and-white print for lining, cut:

1 coat

1 strip, 2" x 4"

From the interfacing, cut:

1 strip, ¾" x 4"

From the white print, cut:

2 pieces, 15" x 18"

From the heavy-duty fusible interfacing, cut:

1 piece, 15" x 18"

From the vinyl, cut:

1 piece, 15" x 18"

From the black print, cut:

72" total of 2¼"-wide bias strips

MAKING THE DOG COAT

This dog jacket has a 4" circumference, which will fit a tiny dog, such as a Yorkshire terrier or a Chihuahua. If you're making a coat for a little bit bigger dog, add ½" to 1" to each strap that goes around the neck and the waist and add to the length by the same amount.

1. Position the ¾" x 4" piece of interfacing on the wrong side of the 2" x 4" piece of lining fabric, ¼" from one long edge. Fuse in place.

2. Fold the fabric rectangle in half lengthwise and stitch a ¼" seam along the long edge. Turn right side out and press flat. Topstitch close to each long edge.

3. Insert the fabric strip through the 1" D-ring and fold the strip so one side is 2" long and the other side is 3" long. Stitch approximately ½" from the fold to secure the D-ring (fig. A).

4. Splay out the two ends of the strip so that the D-ring stands up and position the strip along the center back of the coat. The raw ends will extend beyond the edges of the coat; they'll be enclosed later. Stitch close to each edge to secure (fig. B).

PERSONALIZE THE COAT

What pet owner wouldn't love a custom wardrobe piece for her precious little pet? If you'd like to personalize the jacket with the pet's name you can do so with an embroidery machine or with hand embroidery. Either way, do so now, before the jacket layers are assembled.

5. Position the pink trim along the bottom edge of the coat with raw edges even (the trim is laying on top of the coat fabric). Machine baste in place.

6. Lay the lining fabric on top of the coat fabric, right sides together. Pin. Stitch the layers together using a ¼" seam allowance. Stitch all edges, leaving an opening along the bottom for turning (fig. C).

7. Turn the coat right side out through one of the narrow openings. Roll the seam allowances between your fingers to get them somewhat flat, and then press the coat flat. Take care not to melt the purchased trim!

8. Turn ¼" to the inside at the opening and press. Position the Velcro pieces at each strap end and topstitch in place.

9. Hand sew the flower in place if desired.

10. To make the matching leash, loop one end of the pink webbing through the swivel bolt opening. Fold under the raw edge and stitch the end in place. For the handgrip end, fold back about 6½", folding under ½" of raw edge, and stitch in place (fig. D).

Fig. A

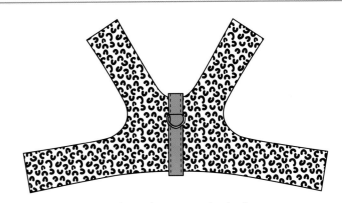

Sew D-ring strip to center back of coat.

Fig. B

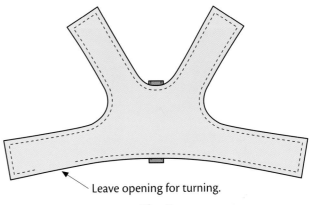

Leave opening for turning.

Fig. C

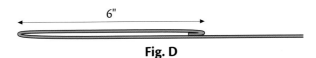

6"

Fig. D

MAKING THE FEEDING MAT

The feeding mat shown was custom made for my dog, Lola. You can personalize the mat with a special pet's name, or simply use more flower appliqués.

1. Using the patterns on pattern page 2, prepare one large flower, one small flower, and one flower center on fusible web. Cut the small flower from pink and the large flower and flower center from black. For the pet's name, you can handwrite the name and enlarge or use a computer font and enlarge to make the name you want. Prepare the name with fusible web.

2. Fuse one 15" x 18" white print rectangle on the heavy-duty interfacing rectangle. This will be the underside of the mat.

3. Fuse the flower layers and the name in place on the remaining white print rectangle.

4. Layer the appliquéd rectangle on the interfacing (the side without the fabric) and smooth in place. Pin around the edges, and then machine baste close to the edge to secure. Repeat with the vinyl rectangle, machine basting it on top of the appliquéd fabric.

5. Use a small plate or saucer as a guide for marking the rounded corners. Cut away the layers on the marked lines (fig. E).

6. Sew the black bias strips together end to end to make one long strip. Fold the strip together lengthwise, right sides together, and press. Apply the binding to the top side of the mat using a ¼" seam allowance. Fold the binding to the back of the mat and topstitch in the ditch to secure all layers.

Cut away corners.

Fig. E

Illustrated Sewing Glossary

Most of the projects in this book are relatively easy—and some are super simple. But if any of the sewing language is unfamiliar, the information provided here may clear things up for you.

Binding. Narrow fabric strips folded over raw edges of projects such as quilts, purse pockets, and more, are called binding. Binding is a neat way to encase and finish edges, especially where there are multiple layers of fabrics and batting. Fold binding strips in half lengthwise, with right sides together. Stitch them to the edge of the project from the right side of the project. Fold the biding strip up at a 45° angle when you reach a corner, and then fold it back down along the next edge of the project and continue sewing.

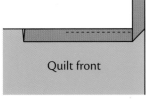

Quilt front

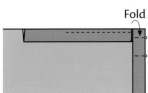

Fold

When you near the starting point, overlap the beginning and ending tails of the binding. Mark the overlap by the same distance as the width of your biding strips. (If your strips are 2½" wide, then mark the overlap to be 2½".) Trim the binding ends to the

marked points, and then sew the ends together with a diagonal seam.

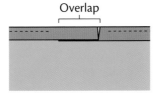

Overlap

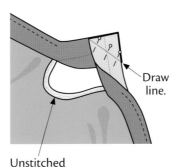

Draw line.

Unstitched quilt edge

Trim the excess fabric corner from the strips, leaving a ¼" seam allowance. Then press the seam allowance and stitch this last bit of binding to your project.

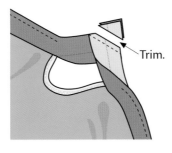

Trim.

Fold the binding over the raw edges of your project and hand stitch in place on the back side.

Clipping curves and inner points. When sewing together parts of a garment that involve curves, it's much easier to make a nice smooth seam if you clip into the seam allowance along the curved edges or into deep points

before turning the pieces right side out.

Clip   Clip   Clip

Snip into seam allowances along curves and at inner points before turning right side out.

Edgestitching. This stitching is done close to the edge of a fabric piece, as the name implies. Try to sew ⅛" or less away from the edge. Usually used when a narrow (⅛" or ¼") edge has been turned under. (See also *Topstitching.*)

Fusible appliqué. A quick-and-easy way to adhere one fabric layer on top of another. Fusible web is applied to the wrong side of the appliqué fabric, the shape is cut out, and then it's ironed onto the background fabric. Decorative machine stitching (such as a satin stitch), worked around the appliqué edges, makes this type of appliqué quite durable, which is especially good for kids' quilts and pillows.

Pressing. When pressing seam allowances, lift the iron before moving it, rather than gliding it back and forth over the fabric. This makes the fabric less likely to become distorted and it keeps your seam allowances from getting caught up in the edge of the iron.

Press, lift, move, and lower the iron along the seam.

Flip top fabric over and press.

Ruching. This term refers to tubes of gathered fabric that are gathered in a zigzag fashion rather than along one edge. When the gathers are pulled tight, the fabric will gather in an S-curve formation, rather than in a straight line, making for a pretty decorative trim.

Mark 1" intervals along one edge of the tube, and then mark 1" intervals along the opposite edge, but offset them by ½" from those on the first edge. Machine baste from one mark to the next as shown, stitching off the edge of the fabric at each mark. Pull the bobbin thread to gather.

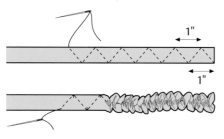

Satin stitching. This stitch can be done by hand to fill in a large area of embroidery, but in this book, I've used machine satin stitching to secure the edges of fusible appliqué. Set your machine to a zigzag stitch (make sure you have an appropriate presser foot in place) and set the stitch width and length to slightly shorter and narrower than the standard setting. Sew around the appliqué shapes with one swing of the needle stitching into the appliqué

shape and the other swing stitching into the background fabric.

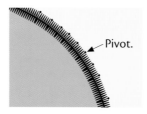

Pivot when needle is outside of the appliqué shape.

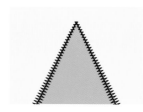

Use a narrower zigzag at points.

Seam allowance. In quilting, a ¼"-wide seam allowance is typically used. In garment sewing, the standard is ⅝". In this book, I used ¼" seam allowances for patchwork, but sometimes used ½" seam allowances on garments or on projects that may be subjected to more stress, like tote bags. If no width is specified, use a ¼" seam allowance.

Topstitching. A little different from edgestitching, topstitching is generally done ¼" away from the edge of the fabric, or ¼" away from a row of edgestitching. Topstitching is decorative whereas edgestitching is more functional for securing narrow edges that have been turned under. Used together,

topstitching can add even more security to an edge or seam, such as on jeans or straps on a tote bag, when the project will be subjected to lots of wear and tear.

Combined edgestitching and topstitching

Zippers. Zippers make great fasteners for closing long openings, such as along the edge of a pillow covering or a long pocket opening in a tote bag or purse. They're relatively easy to install. For a centered zipper, machine baste the opening closed where the zipper will be inserted and press the seam allowance open. Position the zipper tape face down, centering the zipper teeth over the seam line. Pin or machine baste each side of the zipper tape to the *seam allowance only*. Then from the right side of the project, topstitch in place, sewing through the main fabric, the seam allowance, and the zipper tape to secure. Remove the basting stitches along the seam line, and you can open and close the zipper.

Topstitch zipper in place.

Acknowledgments

My gratitude to Mary Green and Karen Soltys of Martingale & Company for valuing the art of the handmade gift.

My love and sincere appreciation to those who dedicated their time and their "heartfelt" passion to helping me make this book into the one I envisioned: Peggy Vicioso, Cheryl Royal, Kim Goodwin, Marcia Wilkie, Darla Sperry, Rachael Lauren (my daughter), and Cheryl Burke and her amazing crew.

A special thanks to Janome America.

About the Author

Beginning with her national debut at the age three on *The Andy Williams Show*, Marie has proven to be a resilient talent with a magnetic presence known across generations. Performing for almost five continuous decades is a rare accomplishment achieved by very few women in the entertainment business.

Marie recorded "Paper Roses" at age 12, earning a Grammy nomination and making history as the youngest female artist to have her debut record go to #1 on the charts.

An additional historic first, Marie became the youngest-ever host of a national television variety show, *The Donny & Marie Show* (1976–81), which became "appointment television" for millions of viewers and was dubbed into 17 languages to be shown around the world. Marie's unique style and fashion ingenuity established her as a monumental trendsetter, which is an ongoing reality today.

On film, Marie starred in *The Gift of Love* (1979), *Side By Side* (1982), and *I Married Wyatt Earp* (1983). She was also in *Goin' Coconuts* (1978), about which she says with a smile, "Some things you never stop paying for!"

In her recording background, among her 27 albums and numerous gold records, an additional career highlight was winning the Country Music Association's "Vocal Duo of the Year" award for "Meet Me In Montana." Her national radio show, *Marie and Friends*, was number one in the markets and her previously annual *Magic of Christmas* tour is a standing-room only event in venues across the country.

Whether performing live for the 2002 Olympics or being in the number-one Superbowl 2003 commercial (a hilarious spoof opposite Ozzy Osbourne), Marie constantly evolves her talents. As well as singing pop and country music, she was also beckoned to the Broadway stage to star in *The Sound of Music* and *The King and I*, which garnered rave reviews and played to sold-out houses on national and international tours. Expanding her musical range even further, Marie has recorded an album of inspirational music featuring operatic-style vocals (to be released in 2010).

Another record-breaking accomplishment, in 2001 Marie became the first-ever celebrity to publicly write about her experience with postpartum depression. Her book *Behind the Smile* was a New York Times best seller. In April of 2009, her next book, *Might As Well Laugh About It Now*, was also an instant *New York Times* best seller.

On season five of *Dancing with the Stars*, 25 million people watched Marie's enthusiasm and determination and her significant weight loss with NutriSystem, and voted her into the finale. Her infamous faint has been replayed millions of times on TV and YouTube, to which Marie responded, "I hit my head so hard when I passed out. . . . I won, right?"

Besides being an international entertainment icon, Marie is a savvy businesswoman. Now celebrating 20 years, Marie Osmond Dolls has received Dolls of Excellence and Doll of the Year (DOTY) awards and nominations, making Marie one of the top doll designers in the world. Marie has also expanded her many business activities into her own line of sewing machines and crafting products as well as a highly anticipated launch with Giftcraft, creating beautiful home-decor products, designer bags, and a popular line of jewelry (Shine!) for QVC.

As cofounder of Children's Miracle Network, Marie helps over 17 million kids every year throughout the U.S, Canada, and Europe, providing state-of-the-art health care and research through 170 children's hospitals. To date, her charity has raised over $3.6 billion with 100% of all funds going to the children. Marie also serves as a spokeswoman for the American Heart Association and "Go Red for Women." In 2009, Marie was honored with a Champion of Children award by the Public Education Foundation and also Nevada Ballet's 2010 Woman of the Year award.

Since 2008, Marie has performed five nights a week to sold-out crowds and great reviews in Las Vegas at the Flamingo Hotel Showroom with her brother Donny. "Donny and Marie" is the first time the duo has reunited on the stage in over 28 years and has also resulted in a new *Donny & Marie* album, released in 2009. Their Vegas contract has been extended to 2012.

Above every other accomplishment, Marie is a proud mother to eight beautiful children who will always be her greatest treasures.

Contact Marie (and send pictures!) at
www.twitter.com/marieosmond or www.facebook.com/marieosmond.